CASTE AWAY

Na. Vanamamalai, affectionately known as Prof. Na. Va, was born on 7 December 1917, in present-day Nanguneri, Tirunelveli district. An active member of the Communist Party of India, he began his career as a schoolteacher in 1942. With other notable figures, he established the Nellai Literary Society in 1947. In 1957, he began studies in folklore, drawing information from the fields of history, sociology, and anthropology. Additionally, he initiated a Tamil research journal titled *Aaraichi*. Despite not being actively involved in university teaching, his extensive contributions to the various research and literary domains earned him the title of Professor. He passed away on 2 February 1980, in Korba, present-day Chhattisgarh.

Joshua Gnanaselvan actively translates plays, short stories, and academic prose from Tamil to English. He is a doctoral researcher at the Department of English and Comparative Literature at the Central University of Kerala, Kasaragod. He served as Assistant Professor of English at Christ (Deemed to be University), Bengaluru, from 2008 to 2015. He specializes in Dalit theatre, Dalit studies, culture studies, and Indian literature.

MISSION STATEMENT

This is an initiative of the Tamil Nadu Textbook and Educational Services Corporation (TNTB & ESC) under the aegis of one of the announcements for the year 2021–22, titled 'Thisaithorum Dravidam' by Honourable Minister for School Education Thiru. Anbil Mahesh Poyyamozhi to identify and translate into English, Kannada, Malayalam and Telugu, Tamil literary works, that they might enhance the reach of Tamil antiquity, tradition and contemporaneity and enrich world literature, and to also translate significant literary voices from other Dravidian languages into Tamil. Both ventures are to be undertaken as either independent or joint publications with collaborating publishers.

Members, Academic Advising Committee (Translation)

1. Dr. R. Balakrishnan, IAS, Researcher and Writer
2. Thiru. S. Ramakrishnan, Writer
3. Thiru. S. Madasamy, Educationist

Project Execution Team

1. Thiru. Dindigul I. Leoni, Chairperson, TNTB & ESC
2. Tmt. R. Gajalakshmi, IAS, Managing Director, TNTB & ESC
3. Dr. P. Kuppusamy, Member Secretary, TNTB & ESC
4. Thiru. D. Mohan, Financial Advisor, TNTB & ESC
5. Dr. T.S. Saravanan, Joint Director (Translations), TNTB & ESC
6. Thiru. G.R. Rajasekaran, Deputy Director (Publications), TNTB & ESC
7. Dr. P. Saravanan, Assistant Director (Publications), TNTB & ESC
8. Thiru. M. Appanasamy, Consultant, TNTB & ESC
9. Tmt. Mini Krishnan, Co-ordinating Editor, TNTB & ESC

CASTE AWAY

PERSPECTIVES ON CASTE-EQUALITY STRUGGLES IN TAMIL NADU

NA. VANAMAMALAI

Translated from the Tamil original
Thamizh Naattil Saathi Samaththuva Poraattak Karuththukkal
by
JOSHUA GNANASELVAN

hachette INDIA

TAMIL NADU TEXTBOOK AND EDUCATIONAL SERVICES CORPORATION
LEARN THOROUGHLY

First published in Tamil in 1980 by People's Publishing Company
This translation first published in India in 2024 by Hachette India
(Registered name: Hachette Book Publishing India Pvt. Ltd)
An Hachette UK company
www.hachetteindia.com

1

ISBN 978-93-5731-732-0 (Paperback)
ISBN 978-93-5731-530-2 (Limited edition hardback)

Hachette Book Publishing India Pvt. Ltd
4th & 5th Floors, Corporate Centre,
Plot No. 94, Sector 44, Gurugram 122003, India

Typeset in Karmina 12/18
by R. Ajith Kumar, New Delhi

Printed and bound in India
by Manipal Technologies Limited

MIX
Paper from responsible sources
FSC™ C043100
FSC www.fsc.org

CONTENTS

TRANSLATOR'S PREFACE

THE CONCEPT OF 'CASTE' CONSTITUTES THE foundational premise upon which the intricate social fabric of India is predicated. It has established a substantial interconnection with 'class', another fundamental construct that shapes the socio-political and cultural ethos. Throughout various historical epochs, numerous figures, including saints hailing from 'lower-caste' communities, monarchs, advocates of social reform, religious leaders, intellectuals, philanthropists, and artists, have actively contested caste-based hierarchies, endeavouring to uplift communities historically marginalized as 'lower' castes. The discourse and manifestations of caste have permeated diverse domains, encompassing religious, social, economic, political, academic, and artistic spheres, as well as the institutions associated therein. The pursuit of caste equality, encapsulated in the titular phrase, has predominantly manifested as a vocal protestation and, to a limited extent, as a token gesture. Primarily, with the exception of a minority, those involved in the endeavour for caste equality often treat it as a verbal platitude, maintaining a certain distance from it as an external construct. The imperative aphorism, 'practise what you preach,' bears minimal weight in their personal domains, as they persist in the practice of endogamy, engage in subtle discriminatory behaviours, and retain their positions of privilege.

I am reminded of Michel Foucault, the twentieth-century French philosopher, best known for his influential work on power, knowledge, and their relationship. Foucault's theory of power challenges conventional notions of authority, urging us to see power as a multifaceted, dynamic force that operates in a decentralized manner throughout society. The essays in this book are carefully woven, drawn from various resources that elevate certain caste groups, and claim the highest space in the caste order by appropriating the scriptures. This claim substantiates the Foucauldian decentralization of power and authority of one group of people or caste. They have added information that supports their social elevation gathered from the Vedas, the Upanishads, the Smritis, archaeological and historical records and verses of saints such as Kapiladeva Nayanar. Each caste group mentioned in this book challenges the conventions of power and authority, the right to perform religious rites, citing the Vedas (both the Aryan and the Dravidian texts), and establishing their communities as the 'top of the twice born' (a phrase used by Gopal Guru in 'How Egalitarian Are the Social Sciences in India?'). The two essays in this book also enumerate instances of the birth of certain castes from a particular cluster.

Professor Na. Va had a prolonged academic engagement. Upon the insistence of his mentor, Professor Karmega Konar, he completed his postgraduate studies in Tamil from The American College, Madurai. What is significant is the profound knowledge he acquired in Sangam literature, the epics in Tamil, and his thorough engagement with writers across the world such as George Gordon Byron, Victor Hugo, Maxim Gorky, and the like. He was proficient in Tamil and English, and the several science essays he translated into Tamil are proof of his linguistic acumen. Earmarked with precision and clarity, his expertise in folklore and engagement in science, history, sociology, and anthropology are visible in his writing. Professor Na. Va's work is based on extensive research. The essays in this book are sourced from ancient Tamil epics (major and minor), temple charters, books on caste histories, and philosophical texts.

I must confess that it was a thoroughly exhilarating experience reading the two essays in this book in their original Tamil version. On the brink of submitting my PhD thesis, I was presented the opportunity to translate this book, which helped me better understand the historicity of caste in Tamil Nadu. While I was excited to engage in this translation exercise, I was fear-stricken for two reasons: the flux one goes through as a translator, staying true to the original as opposed to transcreating the content, and a reverential fear – the stalwart's work I chose to translate. Technological advancements, *Tamil Lexicon*, and a few reference books proved handy in the translation process. It is not without challenges that I completed translating the verses Prof. Na. Va quotes and the archaic language he uses in specific passages.

I thank my dear friend, Dr Thirunavukkarasu M. (pseudonym: Nithin Thiruvarasu) from Chennai, for helping me understand particular contexts and taking me through an imaginative and interpretative world of Tamil verse form.

I thank the Tamil Nadu Textbook and Educational Services Corporation (TNTB & ESC) team for this invitation and the opportunity to contribute to their grand project of translations. I thank the Centre for Learning Futures, Ahmedabad University, for the opportunity to pursue a PGDLT and for shaping me as a translator. I thank my partner Gaana J., PhD, Faculty at IIM, Jammu, for the feedback after reading the draft and helping me finetune a few negligences. I thank my father, Rev. Y. Gnanaselvan, for agreeing to read the draft and offering critical feedback to improve the draft. Thanks to team at Hachette India (especially Sini Sunil and Abhivyakti Singh) for their patience, diligent follow-ups, and for seeing this through. A word of appreciation to Ananya for the meticulous editing and critical comments that helped me calibrate the draft.

Paramathi Velur **Joshua Gnanaselvan**

31 October 2023

EDITORIAL TO THE SECOND EDITION (1999)

[This editorial to the second edition by Me.Thu. Rajkumar of Makkal Veliyeedu was added to the subsequent publication of the Tamil original.]

SINCE PROFESSOR NA. VA'S PASSING, WE HAVE EMBARKED on an endeavour to compile and publish his complete works as an anthology. However, as anticipated, this aspiration has not materialized in the past nineteen years. Despite the collective commitment of numerous research scholars and students of Professor Na. Va towards shared objectives, policies, and principles, it pains me to acknowledge that the publication of his writings has remained stagnant since the release of the initial edition. This project remains incomplete, and I take responsibility for the inaction and express my deep sense of regret for the same. From the outset, I have been overseeing the preparations for publishing his works into anthologies. It is only fitting that I bear the responsibility for falling short of my earlier assurances. Professor Ra. Kamaraj is currently engaged in doctoral research on Professor Na. Va's oeuvre. He has compiled and edited a volume titled *Na Va vin Padaippugal-Nooladaivu* (Works of Na. Va: An Index) that was published by the Centre for Folklore Studies at Palayamkottai St. Xaviers College (Autonomous). Kamaraj's index is not exhaustive – although, it includes details of Professor Na. Va's texts I had intended to compile and publish. Nonetheless, I am confident that the groundwork for the anthology has been established – I can affirm that the undertaking is underway.

Since the compilation process is still underway, we've decided to reissue select writings of Professor Na. Va for the benefit of contemporary scholars' research endeavours. In this regard, Ra. Vasantha, the owner of Makkal Veliyeedu, has pledged to expedite the reissuing efforts. I must admit here that Ra. Vasantha and I share a partnership in life and research pursuits. We want to assure you that Makkal Veliyeedu, with its steadfast principles, remains distinct from recent trends and is committed to expediting the publication of Professor Na. Va's works.

The two essays featured in this book contribute significantly to our fundamental comprehension of caste dynamics in today's context.

If all concerned can discern whom to align with and whom to confront in their pursuit of true emancipation, the struggle for socio-economic transformation will gain even more significant momentum. Unfortunately, the continued discord among those who should be united leaves everyone disadvantaged. It's crucial to remember that certain powermongers have deftly cultivated their self-serving alliances, exploiting the divisions within groups striving against a common adversary. Professor Na. Va provides a lucid and precise explanation of the root cause behind this social divide. It's also noteworthy that these essays were crafted with a keen awareness of the current realities in Tamil Nadu.

27 February 1999 **Me.Thu. Rajkumar**

EDITORIAL TO THE FIRST EDITION (1980)

(This editorial by Me.Thu. Rajkumar of Makkal Veliyeedu [People's Publishing Company] was added to the first publication of the Tamil original [*Thamizh Naattil Saathi Samaththuva Poraattak Karuththukkal*] that informs the readers of the stature of Na. Vanamamalai in the Tamil literary and research landscape.)

A YEAR HAS PASSED SINCE THE UNTIMELY DEMISE OF Professor Na. Vanamamalai, yet his presence lingers among us. His investigative research findings in art, literature, criticism, culture, history, philosophy, anthropology, and folklore have left a lasting impression and established an indelible bond with the reading public, scholars, and his close acquaintances.

His body of work, extensive as it may be, cannot fill the void left behind, particularly for those who were close to him. Despite the excellence enshrined in the hundreds of articles he authored, his insights during private conversations and debates surpassed his published findings. Regrettably, the Tamil community has now lost the opportunity to have his thoughts put into print.

Scholars of Tamil Studies from around the world sought his guidance, and he would dedicate hours, sometimes days, to help them refine their research pursuits, often setting aside his other obligations. Those fortunate enough to have worked under his mentorship continue to reap lifelong benefits. Beyond all else, his colleagues were moved by his compassion, affection, and camaraderie. These factors contribute to the profound sorrow and heaviness felt after his sudden departure. Hence we render it imperative to focus on publishing and disseminating his writings to the public as a tribute to him.

It is customary in the Tamil tradition to release a magazine during the silver jubilee celebration of esteemed individuals – however, Professor Na. Va opted out of this tradition on his 60th birth anniversary in 1978.

Instead, a collection of essays by various scholars was published as part of the commemoration. During the ceremony, I, representing Makkal Veliyeedu, expressed my intention to compile and publish some of his writings in ten volumes. The plan entailed gathering and publishing Professor Na. Va's contributions to various magazines over the years. Subsequently, his writings were assembled, titles for each compilation were settled upon, and details of the collections were made public. Regrettably, only four volumes could be published due to the unavailability of specific old issues and texts; and the challenges compounded by the publishing industry's enduring challenges.

Professor Na. Va, not to downplay my interest but to motivate me, told me, 'Certainly, my volumes deserve to be published, but there's no urgent rush to release them on my sixtieth birthday celebration. Let them come out at a comfortable pace.' In the preface to *Marxist Aesthetics*[1], Na. Vanamamalai wrote:

> Dr. Me.Thu. Rajkumar, who is passionate about literature and a scholar whose dedication lies in historical and sociological research, expressed his intention to publish this volume along with seven

others. Although it's not customary to thank one's foster son, acknowledging his enthusiasm would encourage his endeavours.

Professor Na. Va understood the significant responsibilities I was shouldering at the time. Thus, he penned the above statement to boost the morale of a young individual. However, none of us could have foreseen that the task of publishing his collections would fall upon us at such an unexpected juncture.

After his passing, I believed that creating a comprehensive collection of Professor Na. Va's writings, categorized by domain, would be a valuable endeavour. The research team, too, shared this sentiment. It was an ambitious undertaking to compile all of Professor Na. Va's articles into ten substantial volumes, potentially spanning tens of thousands of pages. The research team stood unanimous in realizing the importance of publishing the works of one of the most exceptional scholars of our time and ensuring the accessibility of his texts. We laboured diligently in order to gather all his contributions to magazines such as *Shakti*, *Saraswati*, *Shanthi*, *Thamarai*, and *Kalaikathir* over the years. Due to difficulties in sourcing specific old issues of these magazines, the compilation process is still underway. We aim to release at least a few volumes by the end of 1981.

Meanwhile, we will release a book of two essays by Professor Na. Va The first essay featured in the inaugural volume of *Aaraichi* (research), whereas the other appeared in the June 1960 issue of *Thamarai* (lotus) [Volume 2, Number 7]. The delay in compilation has further impeded access to his writings for scholars involved in research. Thus, publishing at least a few articles during this ongoing process is imperative. Additional collections may be released later. This book marks the first posthumous publication of Professor Na. Va's work published by Makkal Veliyeedu, without a preface authored by him.

The caste system in Tamil Nadu is intricate and pervasive. Professor Na. Va delved into this subject with his distinctive style. His examination takes a historical perspective, shedding light on the socio-economic underpinnings.

When Makkal Veliyeedu was inaugurated in 1975, he was the first to express reservations only to become the foremost supporter of the endeavour. In a letter, he outlined the complexities of establishing oneself in the publishing industry. He said, 'I hope to see you as a social scientist and a Marxist thinker rather than just a publisher.' In my response, I stressed the significance and necessity of venturing into publishing.

In his subsequent letter, he remarked, 'It's one thing to discuss the pros and cons before embarking on a venture; it's another to lend support once it's underway.' He enclosed a copy of his book titled *Puthukkavidhai Murpokkum Pirpokkum* (New Poetry: Progress and Retrograde) for publication upon my prior request. Subsequently, he provided me with consistent opportunities to publish his works. It is fitting to acknowledge that the support provided by Professor Na. Va laid the groundwork for the evolution of Makkal Veliyeedu into the stable publishing house it is today. We remain dedicated to upholding the legacy of Professor Na. Vanamamalai, his enduring commitment to scholarly pursuits, and the principles he staunchly kept. This, indeed, stands as our profound tribute to him.

Me.Thu. Rajkumar

PERSPECTIVES ON CASTE AND EQUALITY STRUGGLES IN TAMIL NADU

IN THE SOCIAL PROGRESS OF TAMIL NADU, OCCUPATION-based classes emerged as a result of distinction among the various professions.[1] Occupations taken up by generations of individuals came to be called castes. Around second century AD, the upper classes in Tamil Nadu strived to merge the occupation-based groups into the varna system. This type of social establishment was already widespread in northern India.[2] However, it remained a mere superimposition, and occupation was still the basis of determining one's caste. In fact, multiple occupations created an absence of equality among the various classes. Couplet 972, in the ancient Tamil classical text *Thirukkural* by poet and philosopher Thiruvalluvar, is indicative of the inequality.

Transliteration of the Tamil couplet

Puliyur Kesigan, in his *Thirukkural: New Prose Text,* presents the couplet as follows:

Pirappokkum ellaa uyirkkum sirappovva
seythozhil vetrumai yaan [3]

Translation

All humans that live are one in circumstances of birth; diversity in occupation gives each one his special worth.

Explanation

All humans are born equal, yet the treatment they receive varies, since social hierarchy is determined by the occupation one performs.

The exploiting class that did not toil hard imparted caste hierarchy to those involved in various professions, such as the smiths and the farmhands. They not only perceived themselves as superior in relation to the labourers, but also prevented the unification of these labour classes. Their religious and moral texts established the need for and importance of caste hierarchy.

Similarly, when caste-based atrocities, injustices, and pride were at their peak, the oppressed communities struggled in myriad ways. The downtrodden construed several counter arguments and philosophical premises as a response to the ideas and theories that determined caste hierarchy.

The oppressed subverted some of the perspectives enshrined in ancient Vedic texts. Additionally, they manipulated a few interpretations as part of the historical changes.

At the beginning of the twentieth century, several texts elaborated the importance of caste equality.[4] These texts were about people belonging to the lower castes in the social order – the caste system – and considered inferior to all other castes.

Despite the Brahmins' position at the top of the caste hierarchy, as well as stories and legends abounding with the notion that they were superior to all, the lower castes challenged their superiority. Authors such as Manonmaniam Sundaram Pillai, Maraimalai Adigal, V.P. Subbiramaniya Mudaliar, and C.K. Subramaniya

Mudaliar tried to establish their castes as superior.[5] The following texts discuss the struggles faced by the various caste groups to elevate their social standing in a caste-ridden society.

Varuna Sinthamani, published in 1901, explicates the superiority of the Velaalar.[6] The author states that Arya Vedam constituted the Vedas, Upanishads, and Puranas, and Dravida Vedam instituted the Thirukkural and Shaiva Thirumuraigal (Shaivaite compendium). He establishes that there was no evidence for caste distinctions and hierarchies in the Vedas, and the texts that comprised the Dravida Veda.

> In the pre-Vedic times, caste in the Aryan testaments was non-existent. There is no support for caste hierarchy in the Vedas. There is neither support for the exaltation of the Anthanar (Brahmins) nor the debasement of the Shudras. The Vedas do not hinder all the Varnas (castes) from intermingling, inter-dining, and social-give-and-take amongst each other. In the Vedic Suktas, Brahmins, Kshatriyas, Vaisyas, and Shudras emerged as one from the Brahma. This information, too, does not belong to the former edition of the Vedas; they were later additions.[7]

Further, the author of *Varuna Sinthamani* explains that the followers of the Shaivaite tradition perceived themselves superior to the Brahmins, who are followers of the Arya Vedas. He adds that the Velaalar called themselves Vaisyas based on their occupation, and those who laboured for them as Shudras – Vannar (washerfolks), Navidhar (hairdressers), Kuyavan (potters), Thachchan (carpenters), Kollan (blacksmiths), Kannaan (bronzesmiths), Kalthachchan (stone-crafters), Thattan (gold/silversmith), Edayan (shepherd), Chekkan (oil-merchants), Seniyan (weavers), Saanan (warriors), Eruththu Vaniyan (bull merchants), Devadasi Makkal (dancing-girls dedicated to the service of god), Vedan (hunters), Sakkiliyan (leatherworkers, cobblers, and manual scavengers).[8] Thus, *Varuna Sinthamani* states that the Velaalar who followed Shaivism were superior to the followers of the Vedic tradition, the Brahmins. Further, the text mentions that the Velaalar were perceived as Vaishyas based on their profession, while establishing that the Shudras were inferior to the Velaalar. Such perspectives lucidly bring out the contradictions.

In Tamil Nadu, landlords (zamindars) and many landowners with minor landholdings belonged to the Velaalar community. *Varuna Sinthamani* reflects how the Velaalars perceived themselves as being at par with castes above them, whereas, treated those below them as inferior. They did not retaliate against the caste system and were primarily concerned with raising their social standing and appropriated the Tamil texts and the Vedas to elevate themselves.

Around the same time, in 1904, the Gramanis (a sub-caste of the Nadar community), placed by birth into the palm-picking community, amassed wealth by hiring toddy shops and carrying out business. They published *Kshatriyakula Vilakkam*[9] (*The Kshatriya Clan: An In-depth Overview*) to assert their caste superiority. The texts refutes the Gramanis' Shudra identity, proclaiming them as Kshatriyas who accepted the varna system. The book further states that the Brahmins received the higher knowledge of 'Brahman' (Bhramagnanam) from Janakan, a Hindu king of ancient Videha, thus establishing the Kshatriyas as priests to the Brahmins. The author also adds the claim that Gramanis were a part of the military force and refuted their occupation as toddy sellers (a reference made in ancient Tamil texts). The text further elaborates that they were a hardworking community who were neither proud nor denied their lowliness in the social strata. This text may be viewed as an attempt by the rich among the lower castes to educate the members of their community.

In 1937, another text was published that discussed the rise of Southern Nadars: *Nadar Kings and Nayaka Kings.*[10] The authors of this text sets aside the varna system mentioned in the Vedas and the Puranas. The Nadars asserted their superiority and appropriated the word sandror (learned), which was mentioned in Tamil literary works, as a reference to their caste. They claimed that Nadars were professional traders, negating toddy-tapping as their occupation. Most poor Nadars were formerly toddy-tappers, while a small section pursued trading. The text exposes the vested interests of the wealthy business people from the particular section. They claimed themselves to be heirs of the Pandya kings. Instances from the text state that the Nayakas had usurped the country from their ancestors. Since the Nadars were perceived and ranked low in the caste hierarchy, they influenced people similar to their caste and created manifold ideas to attract them in their anti-caste struggles. The preface to *Nadar Kings and Nayaka Kings* states, 'This book is about caste. Since the birth of caste, there has been an agitation to subvert it. "Kabilaragaval"[11] is its proof.' Therefore, the Nadars also tried to find their uniqueness by fabricating new narratives to spread the evolution of their caste.

Similar stories can be found in the folk songs titled 'Nadar Marriage Blessings' that stake the rise of the clan, like in the songs mentioned below:

1. VICTORIOUS *flag commander of the lion engraved flag,*
   Conqueror of Sambaran,[12] Organizer of two Tamil Sangam,[13]
   Holder[14] of Ceylon,[15]
   King[16] of Lankapuri,[17]
   Perumal[18] on the shoulders of the Chetti,[19]
   A monarch of abundance and prosperity,
   The blessed son of Bhadrakali.[20]
2. THE *Numero Uno of the Panchadravidas,*[21]
   Inherently a Pandya,
   Possessor of the Educational Confederate,
   The issuer of sealed currency,
   Son of the Saptha Kanni,[22]
   One who taught Tamil to Guru Muni[23].[24]

The above hymns provide information about the superiority of the Nadar clan. They claim their clan's superiority by appropriating Dasharatha, Rama, and Ravana.

The first hymn states that Dasharatha won against Sambaran (an Asura). Rama won over Eelam (Sri Lanka). Ravana was the king of Lankapuri (Sri Lanka). Thus, they chose their clan leaders by appropriating Puranic tales. Bhadrakali Varapputhiran (Bhadrakali's begotten son from a blessing) and Saptha Kanni Puthiran (son of the seven virgin angels of goddess Shakti) are names of the right-hand caste lineage mentioned in the folk songs titled 'Valangaiyar Saritham' (history of the right-hand faction).

The second hymn addresses that the Valangaiyar (right-hand faction) were born from divine intercourse between Shakti Muni and the Saptha Kanniyar (seven virgin angels). They were nurtured and educated by Bhadrakali. Also, the song claims a kingly/royal lineage by mentioning 'Pandyas by heredity'.

In 1909, *Paravar Puraanam,*[25] a text that celebrates the rise of the Bharatavar – an ethnic group living in Tamil Nadu and Sri Lanka and belonging to a section of the Muthuraja (also known as Mutharaiyar) community – was published. The Bharatavar occupations included pearling, fishing, sand making, and salt production; they lived in the south-eastern coastal regions of Tamil Nadu. Although the author was a Catholic, he acknowledged the Hindu Puranic tales. He presents the community's versions of stories that placed their caste higher and granted it an elevated position in the royal dynasty. The text further states that caste was established by Brahmins, citing the history of Hinduism in this country. Much like the Puranic stories, this text narrates the history of Ariyakula (the Aryan clan) and Kshatriyakula (the Kshatriya clan) kings and explains the history of Chandrakula kings (kings of the Lunar dynasty – Ila, Shashabindu, Pururavan) in the order of father and son, as Urvashi[26] bore Ayu, Nakushan, and Yayati to Chandran, Budhan, and Pururavan. Yayati had many wives. One of them was Devayanai, a seer. Two of her sons were cursed to become Vedar (hunters) for disobeying their father. The eldest son of Sanmishtai,[27] the demon woman, was condemned due to his father's wrath and led his life selling toddy. Likewise, the younger son of Sanmishtai was cursed to become a fisherfolk. Bharatavar originated from him. The text adds that Bharata, who ruled Bharatam in the later years, was their descendant from the male lineage.

Arjuna, a descendant of the Lunar dynasty, married Chitrangatha, the daughter of the Bharatakula (Bharata clan) king, and gave rise to the Pandya dynasty. Thus, the author composed a new myth by associating his community with the legendary kings of ancient times.

Between 1535–37, when the Bharatavar converted to Christianity and practised pearl fishery with the help of the Portuguese to safeguard against the Muslims and the sea pirates, they established a leader among their caste group. They made this leader the unanimous king with the title 'Bharata Pandiyar.' The details of his dynasty are mentioned in the text. It is also emphasized that the superiority of the Bharatavar caste was due to their wealth.

Kilaivalappa Maalai (anonymous) discusses the rise of the Karkathar caste. It provides new mythological stories about its origin, including stories of people such as Vada Malayappa Pillaiyan, who rose to prominence in their clan in the last four hundred years (between the 1500–1900s).

Another community, the Pallars, call themselves

Indrakula Velaalar.[28] Historical texts on the Pallar community allege that they carried rice and sugarcane from *Indraloka*[29] and were praised in the Pandya king's court.[30]

All the myths and narratives created by the various communities referred to in the texts discussed hitherto have a few features in common; taking a closer look at them is vital. The aforementioned texts were written under the influence of the rich in each caste group. They sought to find higher origins for themselves in ancient texts or promoted a higher status for their castes, utilizing ancient sources to develop fresh texts.

The landowning castes claimed that the Arya Veda and the Dravida Veda were distinct traditions and established that the latter held them in high stead. Hence, they approved the varna system and called themselves Vaishyas, while those who laboured for them were termed Shudras. They documented that the Shudras were below them in the caste order. Also they quoted later-day Sanskrit texts to establish themselves at par with castes perceived as higher by citing sources that approved Vaishyas to don power.

Likewise, the Nadars could not find evidence

to prove their caste superiority, and hence, they maintained that the word *sandror* (learned) referred to them. They created new and made-up Puranic stories and claimed they hailed from a kingly tradition and were above the Brahmins and the Vaishyas.

All their perspectives negated the upper-caste status of Brahmins. They rejected the Puranas that established Brahmin superiority. Their texts did not refute the varna system but denied the lowly position granted to their caste. Other than the Velaalar text, *Varuna Sinthamani*, all other texts on caste history approve of the Vedas. They also cite the Vedas to establish caste equality. Even *Varuna Sinthamani* supports the absence of caste distinctions.

Caste history texts that reject the Puranas and the Manusmriti agree with the views of the Vedas. What could be the reason?

Many Vedic hymns originated before the varna system's inception. This is particularly true in the first part of Rig Veda. At that time, the Aryans eked out a living as pastoral tribes.[31] Class and caste were non-existent. Hence, equality prevailed among the masses. They worshipped natural forces as their deities. Therefore, these hymns of the Rig Veda do not mention any evidence of caste hierarchy.

Then, why do these caste histories reject the Puranas and the Manusmriti? The Puranas and the Manusmriti emerged when it became necessary for the upper classes to bring in class distinctions, institute the varna system and stabilize caste divisions. The purpose was to justify caste hierarchy and lay down legal rules.

To fulfill the primary goal of creating class distinctions, the upper classes wrote down the Puranas and the Manusmriti to institutionalize the varna system. Therefore, those castes that demanded caste equality rejected the perspectives of these texts.

These castes cited the Vedas to prove they were equal to the Brahmins. They engaged in two types of research to counter the Puranic myths. One: They pointed out the contradictions in the Puranas and the contradiction in one Purana against another. Second: To back their claims, they chose the *Manimekalai*,[32] a Buddhist text, and the *Neelagesi*,[33] a Shaivite text – both these texts opposed the Puranic perspectives. The perspectives offered in *Manimekalai* and *Neelagesi*, which refute the superiority of the Brahmins in the varna system through the exposition of several saintly sources, bolstered the views of caste historians.

Furthermore, 'Kabilaragaval', a song from an

early eighteenth century composition, helped the historians immensely. This song establishes that birth does not determine one's status as hierarchically higher or lower. According to 'Kabilaragaval', Aadhi, a Pulaichi (Pulaya woman; a lower caste in the caste hierarchy, formerly an untouchable community), and Bhagwan, a Brahmin, bore seven children – Kabilar, Valluvar, Auvai, Athiyaman, Uruvai, Valli, and Uppai. Among them, Kabilar grew up in the Andanar (Brahmin) clan, Valluvar in the Parayar clan, Auvai in the Paranar (Panar – an ancient musical community similar in social stature to that of Paraya and Pulaya) clan, Athiyaman in the kingly clan, Valli in the Kuravar clan (a de-notified criminal tribe of the Kurunji [mountain] regions), Uppai in the Vannar clan, and Uruvai in the Nadar clan.[34] Though different clans raised them, they were admired by the general public, especially people who lived a superior lifestyle. Caste is not the benchmark to determine one's status as higher or lower. This song emphasizes that education determines one's superiority and inferiority. Apart from 'Kabilaragaval', other texts written between the sixth and tenth centuries, such as Siddha songs and Saint Thirumoolar's 'Thirumandiram' (holy incantation), strengthened the perspective of caste equality.

Siddha songs such as 'What is Caste?' and 'What is Religion?' served as a war cry to people perceived as lower castes.

Thus, the communities discussed so far have collected varied sources from Sanskrit and Tamil texts and formulated diverse perspectives, protesting against caste-based societal ups and downs.

Recently, I accessed a text that contributed immensely towards such struggles on caste equality titled *Judgment of Adalat Court, Chittoor*.[35] The text is in two parts – the first covers the 'Dispute between Panchangam Gundaiyan and Markasagayam Aasaari' and the second 'The pleadings and final adjudication of the case involving the parties Markasagayam Aasaari and Co., representing the plaintiffs, and Gundaiyan and Co., representing the defendants.'

The Aasaari community, also known as Panchakarma, identified themselves as Vishwa Brahma (artisans), who have endured years of caste-based oppression. Historical records (charters)[36] confirm that during the Chola dynasty, the 'right-hand caste clusters collectively decided to ostracize the Panchakarmas from their habitat. The predominant practices amongst the Panchakarmas are Udan Koottam (coexistence) – engaging in rituals, celebrations, and participating in village gatherings, and the act of Oor vilakku (banishment) that resembled the contemporary practice of Saathi Vilakku (caste-based ostracization/untouchability). The Panchakarmas belonged to the left-hand caste cluster,[37] primarily constituting a working-class community. One of the charters asserts that the landlords subjected the Panchakarmas to numerous injustices. Multiple records confirm that the left-hand caste cluster, comprising ninety-six communities, united in resolute opposition against these injustices.[38] These working-class communities have endured unceasing cruelties from the upper castes. However, an in-depth analysis of this historical context lies beyond the scope of this article.

The Panchakarmas were skilled artisans who took up the following five professions: ironsmith (Kollar), carpentry (Thachchar), sculptor (Kal Thachchar), coppersmith (Kannar), and goldsmith (Thattar). Despite their diverse professions, they were a closely knit community, sharing the rights to trade, socialize, and make a living through various occupations.

Ironsmiths supplied essential items such as ploughs, swords, sickles, and writing instruments to the farmers, warriors, and scholars respectively. Carpenters crafted tools from wood and provided carpentry work needed for construction, irrespective of caste. Sculptors, serving as architects or stone masons, played a crucial role in developing art and architecture, creating magnificent palaces and temples. Goldsmiths fashioned ornaments, coins, and amulets, contributing significantly to the refinement of civilization and the growth of commerce. Coppersmiths specialized in crafting copper vessels and tools indispensable for all sections in the social hierarchy.

The upper castes viewed these artisans as dutiful Shudras, valued for their service. At the same time, Brahmins perceived hard work as disdainful, and exploitative landlords saw the artisan groups as a subjugated class destined for servitude.[39] Therefore, the Brahmins and landholders framed several perspectives to cement this notion.

The hardworking Panchakarmas (artisan communities) retaliated against these atrocities. They fought against the injustices and struggled for caste equality. During their strife, they developed novel ideas and pioneering ideological standpoints that drew from ancient sources that vouched for caste equality.

The abovementioned case (*Judgment of Adalat Court, Chittoor*) emerged due to such a commotion. The issue at stake was the right to solemnize a wedding: did the right to solemnize an Aasaari community wedding lie with the Brahmins or the elders from the Aasaari community? This is illustrated in the following extract from the *Judgment of Adalat Court, Chittoor*:

> At Sathurppperi, in the Chittoor district, Panchangam Gundaiyan and a gang of Brahmins gathered and objected to the wedding solemnized by Sagayam Aasaari from the priestly class of the Vishwa Brahma lineage. The wise men who gathered there under the auspices of Panchangam Gundaiyan instructed that they could continue with the wedding ceremony in the presence of their clan preceptors without the aid of Panchangam Gundaiyan if Sagayam Aasaari could answer all the questions posed by Panchangam Gundaiyan from the Vedic texts. The deal was that if he failed to answer correctly, Panchangam Gundaiyan must solemnize the wedding. The Panchayat was summoned, and a dispute broke out between

Panchangam Gundaiyan and Markasagayam Aasaari in the presence of the Panchayat.

Upon hearing Markasagayam Aasaari's deposition, the Panchayat elders rendered their verdict in his favour, as he had addressed all the questions posed by Gundaiyan in the Vedic texts correctly. The essence of the arguments put forth by Markasagayam Aasaari in that conversation is encapsulated in the subsequent court affidavit, which I will refrain from stating here. The judgment read thus:

> Due to Pandit Markasagayam Aasaari's adept presentation of perspectives from the Puranas, which were easily understood by all present, and his dexterous defence that left you baffled and dumbfounded, it is now incumbent upon Panchangam Gundaiyan and his assistants to abstain from disrupting the wedding ceremonies rooted in the Vedas conducted by the Vishwa Brahma clan.

Defying the verdict, Gundaiyan and his accomplices turned to aggressive methods. Markasagayam Aasaari lodged a petition in the Magistrate's court. Supported by witnesses' testimony, the Magistrate imposed fines on

Gundaiyan and his associates. Additionally, he directed the claim for damages resulting from the disruption of the wedding to be presented in the Civil Court.

In 1814, Markasagayam Aasaari and his colleagues filed a complaint in the Chittoor District Adalat Court. The arguments presented by the petitioners, including Gundaiyan's response and the final verdict, have been extensively documented. Therefore, providing a comprehensive account of the entire judgment in this context is permissible. Given that the initial part of the Markasagayam Aasaari vs. Gundaiyan dispute elucidates the discussions between the plaintiff and defendant within this ruling, we will focus solely on the omitted elements subsequently.

The Brahmins should not prevent
the Vishwa Brahma clan from solemnizing weddings
according to the Vedic tradition

Chittoor District
Adalat Court Judgment

A true copy of the original dated 1814.
Judgment in original No. 205, 1818.

Plaintiffs

Residents of Sathurpperi:

Vellai Aasaariyaar
Markasagayam Aasaariyaar
Rudra Aasaariyaar
Venkitachala Aasaariyaar
Nallaa Aasaariyaar
Kuzhandai Aasaariyaar
Chinnakkannu Aasaariyaar
Arunachala Aasaariyaar
Mahadeva Sthapathiyaar
Dakshinamoorthi Sthapathiyaar
Varada Achariyaar

Counsel: Abdul Ayub

Documents produced by the Plaintiffs include details of the Veda Shastras found inside file No. 1:

a) Yajur Veda
b) Purushashuktham
c) Moolasthambam
d) Vachirasoosi
e) Vemanabathyam
f) Kabilaragaval
g) District Magistrate's Verdict Report

Defendants

Residents of Sathurppperi:

Panchangam Gundaiyan
Arunachala Aiyan
Venkatasubbu Shastry
Vishwathi Shastry
Thottachary
Yekkiya Theetchathar
Viyasa Pattar
Suryanarayana Shastry
Joshi Shastry
Vandavasi Sirastharayyar

Counsel: Arunachala Mudali

The Defendants produced no documents.

Trial witnesses

Aandiyappa Mudali
Sankaranarayana Reddy
Gobi Chetti
Appasamy Pillai
Venkatasubbu Nayakkan

Plaintiffs' Complaint

The Vishwakarmas asserted their Brahminical lineage from the rishi gotras, tracing it through the advent of Sanagarishi gotra (involved in ironsmith works); Sanathanarishi gotra (involved in carpentry works); Abunasarishi gotra (involved in bronze smith works); Prathanasarishi gotra (involved in stone works); and Suparnasarishi gotra (involved in gold smith works), the descendants of Brahmarishis, creations of Panchamuga Brahma (five-faced Brahma). As the wedding ceremonies were about to commence in the homes of the first, second, and third plaintiffs, it was customary to recite the Paathiya Shruti. However, the defendants, who belonged to the Shankara caste, entered provocatively and disrupted the proceedings, denying the plaintiffs the right to conduct the wedding according to Vedic rites. They insisted that only they had the authority to conduct the marriage according to the Puranas. They gathered a group and physically assaulted the plaintiffs. The incident was documented, and a formal complaint was filed with the District Magistrate. The Magistrate conducted an inquiry based on the plaintiffs' grievance and meted out an appropriate punishment to the defendants.

Additionally, he provided a copy of the case report to the District Civil Court and recommended a fine to compensate for the incurred losses. Consequently, the defendants were directed to pay a sum of ₹550 for the wedding expenses. In light of these events, the plaintiffs deemed it necessary to establish that the defendants were prohibited from entering any of the Vishwakarma villages during auspicious ceremonies.[40]

Defendants' Response

The defendants responded that the plaintiffs, lacking any connection to the Brahmarishis, as alleged in the complaint, were not affiliated with the Brahma Saint clan and were considered equal to the Panchamas (people who belonged to the lowest strata of the caste society; the ex-'untouchables'). This status precludes them from assuming the role of Vedic teachers, as their occupation was viewed as lowly. In contrast, as per the Shrutis, the defendants originally belonged to the Brahmin caste. According to the varna order, every caste below them was responsible for various other duties, and their job was to perform rituals. The plaintiffs chose to deviate from the customary practice by conducting the wedding and, as a result, suffered no discernible loss.

Plaintiffs' Rejoinder

The plaintiffs replied that Saanaga Saint took the form of Manu Brahma, Sanaathana Saint manifested as Maya Brahma, Prathnasa Saint embodied Shilpi Brahma, and Supernasa Saint was represented as Vishwagna Brahma. They were descendants of those initially divided into these categories of Brahmarishis, and there were numerous other rishis in this ancestral line.

According to the ancient Brahminic Vedic texts, Manu Brahma is linked to the iron industry, and Dhuvasta Brahma to the copper industry, as stated in the hymns of the Rig Veda. Vishwagna Brahma is associated with the gold industry, as specified in the Sama Veda and Pranavadeva recitation. Through the performance of these five moral actions (the above-stated occupations), these principles contribute to preserving the world.

The Vishwakarmas energized by igniting the five metals, such as gold, silver, copper, iron, and the nine crystals (pearl, diamond, vitriol, gem, emerald, sapphire, sardonyx, topaz, and coral). They created their worshipping vessels, armaments of various sorts, missiles and weapons for those who approach, etc., adorable ornaments for God and sacred places, thrones, and raised mounds – for destruction, darkness, and grace; in other words, for all auspicious and inauspicious occasions.[41]

The plaintiffs, who trace their lineage to Manu Brahma and Maya Brahma, namely Dhuvasta Brahma, Shilpi Brahma, and Vishwagna Brahma, assert their entitlement to impart teachings through the recitation of the Panchanga (almanac). They affirm their Brahmin status based on their birthright as descendants of Vishwakarma.

In contrast, the defendants share the exact birth origin within the Nishada (lower) castes, such as Paraya, Sakkili, etc. The verses from the Manusmriti serve as irrefutable evidence supporting the plaintiffs' claim.

The lineage of revered Saints has a fascinating diversity in its origins. Kalaikkoattaar, known for his sanctity, was born to a deer; Kaadhi Maharaja was the forebearer of Kausigar (Vishwamitran); Jambunar, famed for his cunningness, hailed from a fox; Gauthamar emerged from a cow; Valmikar, belonging to the Agastiyar lineage, was born to a huntress;

Viyasar's origins trace back to a fisherwoman; Vasishtar, esteemed as one of the Seven Saints,[42] was taken of a *Dasi*, signifying a devotee or female disciple; Naradar's birth was attributed to a washerwoman; Kaundinyan's lineage stemmed from a widow; Mathangar, revered as a Saint, was born to a Sakkiliya woman (a lower caste); Mandavyar, also known as Adimandavya Rishi, was delivered of a frog; Saankiyar's lineage was attributed to a Paraya woman; Kaarkeyar, recognized as a Saint, emerged from a donkey; and Sounagar, esteemed as a Saint during the era of Atharva Veda, was born of a dog. Notably, Vemana, a prominent Telugu Saint, was born into the Paraya clan as a consequence of adhering to specific dietary restrictions. It is worth mentioning that Vemana later incurred censure upon the Paraya. Yet, is there a need for more knowledge regarding the initial birth in this lineage? Koodaththi bore Vasishta, akin to the twice-born (Brahmins) of the red-water lily. Sandali, Vasishta's wife, bore Saththiyar, while Paraasarar (one of the ancient Indian sages who authored Vishnu Purana) was borne by the Pulaichi (a lower-caste woman) of Punganur (a municipality in Chittoor district). A fisherwoman delivered Vedaviyasa to Paraasarar, and all the above saints were born into the Shankara caste, also perceived as lower castes.[43] The Court has examined this evidence and confirmed that the defendants are descendants of the above Saints.

The Court has also examined the rejoinder of the defendants; despite the production of the above list of saints by the plaintiffs in their reply, if it is true that there is a Vedic verse that indicates that the plaintiffs are descendants of Brahma, there is no way that the Puranic texts such as Bharata would place them in a lowly status. The kings have acknowledged that the plaintiffs are Shresthas (noblemen) and have foregone universal grants for a long time.

Judicial Ruling

1. When the court examined and consulted all the proofs from the Vedic Shruti mentioned in this case number, they approved that the plaintiffs are from the Vishwa Brahma clan and that the defendants belong to the Shankara caste.
2. The contention that the plaintiffs, belonging to the Panchamas (outcastes), can be accurately identified as such, as asserted in the response that

the defendants are of Brahmin caste, does not entail an infringement of the prevailing Shastras. This is posited without invoking any scriptural verse for conciliation and without alleging any alternative disposition by the plaintiffs.

3. Upon scrutinizing the saints' births in connection to the defendants' lineage through the Puranas, it becomes evident that they trace their origins to the Shruti recitals of *Vachirasusi* (the original divine institute of caste) and the Brahmin sage Vemana, as attested by both the defendants and the plaintiffs in their responses. The plaintiffs assert that the fifteen saints enumerated by the defendants do not belong to their genealogy. Interestingly, the defendants, when questioned, do not contest this assertion. They acknowledge that their saints emerged from the Brahma Beej.[44] It is inconceivable that Brahma, a divine figure, would not align himself with lower castes and animals, as it would contradict natural justice. Therefore, if this assertion holds, it stands to reason that the saintly sources should not be at odds with the accounts presented in the Puranas.
4. To make it known that the origin of the Brahmin

lineage is said to be different from the Shastra origin, the origin of the fifteen saints mentioned above must have also been established by presenting the 'Sahasranama' (Sanskrit hymn) before the said District Chaturameen Pandit. Also, all the sages were born after the varnas were established in the world order. No evidence is found that defendants who descended from the legacy of such saints belong to the Brahma clan, born at the beginning of creation.

5. If the defendants, being Brahmins, are considered superior to all other varnas, then it implies the need for karma, which is the ultimate source of all existence and somewhat akin to the force of creation of Brahma. Without this notion, they would not seek sustenance humbly, leading a life reminiscent of the Jangamas (nomads).
6. On examination of the Veda Shastras filed by the plaintiffs as documents, it was found that not even one letter or a word from the Vedas in the hymnal recitation of the defendants is the same as that of their predecessors – the sages. Since the defendants are the descendants of the lower-caste ancestral saints, acknowledging them as universal masters/

superiors is a sheer lack of scientific inquiry and ignorance. But in the past, somehow, they engaged in gambling, cheated ignorant and reckless ones enslaved by a few nations, and have exercised their authority over those enslaved people to date. Finding out about such scams, knowing about the Varunashrama Dharma (classification of human societies according to their caste – born out of one's profession), and taking corrective measures lies at the behest of the Honourable Government.

7. The plaintiffs argue in their plea and response that they are the descendants of the Panchamuga Brahma. They asserted that they maintained the cosmic order and diligently performed the prescribed rituals, known as Brahma Karma, by the Shrutis and based on the Samasthaas. They claim the same to be in line with the teachings of the Yajur Veda, aiming to safeguard the world. Much like the omnipresent nature of air, they assert that all, including animals, witness their actions. They argue that ample evidence supports their claim as the rightful descendants of the esteemed Brahmin lineage.

8. Unable to bear the praiseworthiness of the Vishwa Brahmas in legends such as Bharata, the defendants

have portrayed the Vishwa Brahmas malignantly through fabricated narratives. However, there is no scope for fables in the Puranas since they are the Adi Vedas and bore witness to all scriptures that hold a superior position.

9. During the trial, it was evident that the defendants compelled the plaintiffs to gather and impeded them from conducting the wedding ceremony. According to the Magistrate's diary, the defendants were ordered to compensate the plaintiffs with ₹550 for the damages incurred, including the costs of the ransacked groceries meant for the wedding feast. The plaintiffs were supported by witnesses, including Nagojirao, Subburaya Mudali, Venkatarama Nayakkan, and fifteen others. The diary also stipulates that the plaintiffs have the rightful authority to perform their marriage rituals by Vedic rites. Additionally, the defendants were explicitly instructed not to enter the plaintiffs' premises or disrupt their ceremonies.

Accordingly, dated 15 December 1818
Verdict of Chittoor District Court
A true copy of the original

* * *

The above case details and judgment regarding the battle for caste equality unmistakably present the perspectives of proponents and opponents of this pursuit. Advocates for equality draw upon the Yajur Veda as their foundational text. The surge in productive capabilities during the era of Yajur Vedic hymns, in contrast to the preceding Rig Vedic period, can likely be attributed to the advent of metal and wooden tools. With the aid of these implements, humanity progressed towards a more affluent existence, markedly improving upon the lifestyle followed during the Rig Vedic era.

During the Rig Vedic era, people venerated natural elements as deities. However, in the Yajur Vedic period, a shift occurred, and they began to revere their creative endeavours as gods, such as Brahma and the five-faced Brahma, along with the Pancha Krithyas representing their creative achievements. In the later verses of the Rig Veda, particularly in the 'Purusha Sukta' (believed to be a later addition), there was an attempt to elucidate the origin of the universe and its inhabitants, influenced by the interactions of people dining together. Offering oblations became a collective form of worship, solidifying emotional bonds among individuals in a community way of life.

The 'Purusha Sukta', that originated during the early stages of the varna system, has been interpreted by later sects to convey notions of superiority and subjugation among different varnas. It underscores the idea that all varnas are ultimately derived from a common material essence. I have included specific sections of the 'Purusha Sukta' that elucidate the origins of the varnas, as they are crucial to this essay.[45]

* * *

Rig Veda

Eighth Benefit

'Purusha Sukta'

Irudi (a seer): Narayanan
Devathai (a deity): Virat Purushan (unparalleled energy)
Santhasu (Science of Vedic prosody): Anushkubu in the beginning and Dhirustibu at the end
Vishayam (Topic): Creation

The Sorubam (Nature) of Virat Purush

Virat Purush is characterized by a thousand heads, eyes, and limbs, embodying a formidable ten-feet presence encompassing the world. Purush is all-pervading, bearing responsibility for the plenitude of cereal crops. His magnificence is marked by nobility and eminence. A quarter of the universe constitutes his being, while the imperishable and self-illuminating entities comprise three-fourths of his essence.

Initially, three-fourths of Purush's essence remained in a state of purity. One-quarter of his existence assumed an illusory form, encompassing the facets of creation, preservation, and dissolution. Following this transformation, he engendered the cosmos from absolute annihilation. The universe emanated from the Supreme Being. Purush emerged as a corporeal manifestation of this expansive cosmos. This soul, characterized by its Virat nature, eventually assumed a divine form. Subsequently, he brought forth the terrestrial realm and fashioned corporeal vessels for earthly entities.

Then, the gods performed a yagna (sacrifice). The spring season was its ghee, summer was its firewood, and winter was its oblation. Surrounding the altar were seven sacrificial pits, and three times seven pieces of firewood were also placed. When the gods performed the yagna this way, Purush was tied like a sacrificial cow.

On the pyre, they offered the first-born Purush as sacrifice. The gods, Saadhyas, and saints accepted him as a magnificent offering. Curd and ghee were derived from the universal sacrifice. Using the vital air from the countryside and the woods, Purush created angelic animals, and the Rig, Sama, and the Yajur Vedas, and Gayathriyathithi (prosody) also came into existence. Also, horses, animals with two rows of teeth, cows, sheep and goats were created.

In the sacrificial act, how many pieces was Purush divided into? What did the arms transform into? And what were his thighs and feet named after? His face embodied the Brahmin, his arms embodied the Kshatriya, his thighs created the Vaishya, and his feet gave rise to the Shudra. From his heart, the moon emerged, and from his eyes, the sun was born. Indra (sun) and Agni (fire) took form from his face, while Vayu (air) originated from his breath. From his navel emerged the mid-air or open space, the sky formed from his head, earth from his feet, and directions from his ears. This is how the world came into existence.

* * *

These passages recount the ancient tale about the creation of the world. These hymns likely originated during a period marked by the proliferation of small, distinct groups and the emergence of specialized tasks. These ethnic communities, predominantly pastoral in nature, practised rituals such as yagna and yaga to forge unity. Yagna was conducted on a modest scale, while larger assemblies engaged in yaga. Every essential aspect of life was accompanied by a yagna venerating various natural forces in the bygone eras. As society progressed, perspectives expanded, leading to the conception of a myth that envisioned the genesis of the world alongside the advent of specialized tasks known as 'Purusha Sukta'.

The Rig Vedic teachers offered cows, goats, and horses in sacrifice, believing that this would increase their herds of these animals. They also made offerings of man to increase the human population. Through these actions, they believed they could attain their desires. These practices are still observed among some ethnic groups in Tamil Nadu. They held the conviction that the creation of the universe was linked to each human sacrifice. Additionally, they believed this human sacrifice led to the division of the once-unified society into four groups. 'Purusha Sukta' is the product of this artistic expression. Within this framework of thought, there was no inherent notion of superiority or subjugation among the various classes.

Only after completely breaking away from the industrial production system did Brahmins and Kshatriyas begin to evaluate labour as inferior and thought superior. As a result, they treated labourers as inferior and believed they were born to work under them – reducing their stature to that of slaves. The Puranas and Manusmriti emerged during this period, establishing caste superiority and inferiority. In the meantime, the intermingling of various varnas saw the birth of Shankara castes. Many rishis arose in the lineage within the Shankara castes and wrote many Puranas. They delved into rishi sources (Vedas and Upanishads) and concluded that excellence is determined by God (Brahma) given knowledge, not by one's birth.

Earlier in this essay, it was established that varna distinction is not mentioned in the hymns of the Rig Vedic period, where cohabitation was prevalent. Yajur Veda portrays creative power as Brahma. The Vishwa Brahmas tried to establish their equality and supremacy upon this premise.

Also, the Brahmins loathed the smiths' occupations since they worked with iron, wood, and copper. They found the smiths despicable. However, the artisan communities tried to establish their caste ascendancy by claiming that their works led to world security and were the occupations of the Brahma. To establish this, they projected the five artisan groups[46] as heads of the smiths and initiated themselves as successors of the clan.

They dismissed the viewpoints of people (Brahmins) who prioritized rationality and viewed certain occupations as less esteemed. Instead, they highlighted the idea of valuing labour, seeing it as a virtuous act that sustains the world, akin to the noble deeds of God. This perspective is unique to their caste's history and not found elsewhere.

Henceforth, both sections quote from the Puranas. Brahmins argued that texts such as Bharata blaspheme the Brahma, and many Puranas refer to Pancha Karumis (the five smiths) as equal to Panchamar (the fifth caste, the 'lowest').

The Brahmins stated that the rishis born from the Brahma have no link with the Pancha Karumis. They quoted the Manusmriti to show evidence of the five smiths' inferior status.

But the smiths used the stories of the rishi origin drawn from the same Puranas to slander the Brahmins and prove that their clan had no specialties.

Of the two schools of thought that emerged to defend and oppose the caste system, the Brahmins supported it, while the smiths opposed it.

Apart from the court documents mentioned above, other significant arguments are found in the Thiruvenkata Mudaliar's 'Chittoor High Court Verdict' that elaborates on the Gundaiyan vs. Markasagayam Aasaari dispute.

Let us briefly examine the essence of the debate about their sects and morals, and the nature of the perspectives exemplified in that dispute.

We have seen that Markasagayam Aasaari et al. mentioned in their petition that the Yajur Veda says the five smiths originated from the Panchamuga Brahma (five-faced Brahma). They also shared documents that discuss the excellence of their professions. Markasagayam Aasaari explained in his 'argument' that their occupations are the works of the gods, and he quoted from Yajur Veda to substantiate the same:

> *The Chittoor Adalat Court Judgment* documents the fact from Yajur Veda, stating that the five Vishwakarma communities hailed from the five-faced Brahma. Umamaheshwaran alias Rudran is the creation of Manu Brahma (iron industry); Vishnu, who possesses the character of Narayana, hails from Maya Brahma (carpentry); Shri Hiranya Karpa Brahma is a creation of Dhuvasta Brahma (copper industry); Devendran born out of Shilpa Brahma (gold industry); and Savita Bhaskaran alias Surya is a creation of Vishwagna Brahma (stone masonry). (Mudaliar)

Here, Markasagayam Aasaari states that Brahma and other Vedic Gods are performers of various occupations. The purpose of the Brahmins who did not engage in any labour was to show that they were not the descendants of the non-occupational Gods.

The Manusmriti prescribes the Shudras to be subservient to the three upper castes. They do not possess the right to wisdom. They have no right to recite the Vedas or hear them.

But when Gundaiyan queries about the destiny of each varna, Markasagayam Aasaari details the following about the Shudras:

The Rule for Shudras: In the beginning, the Vishwa Brahma clansmen divided the earth into five parts – Kurunji (mountainous region), Paalai (dry lands), Mullai (forests), Neithal (seashore), and Marutham (cropland) – and gave them to the Shudras, who, in turn, learned about the suitable crops to be grown at specific times and cultivated accordingly, saving the lives of people. The Shudras also provided eternal sustenance to the gods and followed the rules of the scriptures.

Answering the next question, Markasagayam Aasaari says that the Shudra also has the right to study the Vedas. By saying this, he argues that all varnas and castes are equal.

Since the Puranas carry supporting and opposing arguments of varna, Markasagayam Aasaari points out the many versions of the Puranas and says that all of them are false. After narrating several mythological stories and pointing out their contradictions, Markasagayam Aasaari says:

> In the Bhagavata and other Puranas, it is recounted that Adisakti emerged from Vishnu's navel, giving rise to Shiva, who is Vishnu's father. In the Macha Purana, Rudra is described as being created by Brahma. At the same time, in the Naratiya Purana, Brahma is depicted as appearing on Narayana's right, Vishnu on his left, and Shiva in the middle. In the Linga Purana, Shiva manifests as Rudrakaram before Brahma, causing Vishnu and Lakshmi to appear on his sides and Brahma and Saraswati on his right. Due to Brahma's slight lapse in concentration, Rudra, born from Brahma's sigh, steps in to complete the task. Afterward, Brahma resumes the work on his own. This results in the transformation of one Shakti into three distinct entities. It is also mentioned that Lakshmi, Saraswati, and Kali were born in this divine form; isn't it true?
>
> If yes, listen, Mr Gundaiyan! Now that I have made it clear, do you and your acquaintances have any doubt in my explanation of the myths and legends

> in Bhagavata, Markandeya Purana, Varaga Purana, Narathiya Purana, Linga Purana, etc., as mere myths? (Mudaliar)

Thus, he vehemently disproves everything by pointing out mythological contradictions to counter stories that teach superiority and subservience.

Gundaiyan illustrates the dietary habits followed in every Brahmin household to show that the Brahmins are a superior clan: 'Everyone eats in our household, whereas no one eats at your house!'

In response, Markasagayam Aasaari says:

> Panchang Gundaiyan! You who belong to the fold of the Panchamas (the lower castes), but you saw that no one ate in your house in the past; you caught fools and traitors who roamed about without Vedic investigation, cheated them by gambling, and enslaved them, disguised yourself as Brahmarishis, amazed everyone with your upper caste tricks, tricked the Viswakarmas and fools into believing in your precepts, and established that the king's dependents are right-handed and the working class Kammalar as left-handed and ensured that the left-

hand cluster did not dine with the right-hand cluster, and eventually, ensured that everyone inter-dined from your home. Back then, people who did not know your community status inter-dined with you, yet the Rajputs, Pontilis, Lalas, Kusilathiyars, Marathas, Kannadiyars, Veerashaivars, Jaina Velaalars, Pattu Nurkars, Saaththaniyars, Valluvars, Tulukkars, Malukkars, etc., who knew your family lineage, still do not eat in your house, isn't it? But nowadays some people who don't know you eat from your house. Why do the Pancha-Gauda and Pancha-Dravida (two significant groupings within the Brahmin fold) not dine at your home? Nothing but the fact that you are backward; even if some castes eat from your house based on your indoctrination, their belief that you are a Brahmin will not make it true. So, if you are a Brahmin, you should do at least one of the Pancha krityam (the five smith occupations)! Who will agree that you are the lineage of Brahma without knowing any profession and wandering around like Jogi and performing Yagna like Jangamma (Jogis and Jangammas are mendicants)? Those who know the truth will never agree, won't they? (Mudaliar)

Here, there is a discussion on dietary habits. According to Markasagayam Aasaari, the Brahmins prohibited people from eating with a person belonging to another caste. Further, he mentions the history of Idangai (left-hand castes) and Valangai (right-hand castes).[47] Some of the Chola period's charters help us to understand the nature of these divisions. T.N. Subramanian says:[48]

> The Tiruchirappalli Aduthurai inscription narrates the injustices meted out to the 96 castes of the *Idangai* (left-hand) caste group by the Vanniyar, Velaalar, Brahmins, etc., with the help of government officials. Similarly, inscriptions from various parts of the country inform the tax burdens the *Idangai* (left-hand) caste group bore back then. An inscription traced from Aavani in Mysore is of great importance. It conveys the conclusions arrived at by representatives of the people who complied with the king's mandate. Since the beginning of the Chola dynasty, taxes on cows and buffaloes were not levied on the 78 regions of the Nigarili Chola region (a division in Mysore when it formed a part of the Chola dominion) and the 48,000 lands under the Jayankonda Chola region (renamed after the Cholas victory from the Pallava

> kings). The officials decided to levy the taxes imposed by King Madhuranthaga Muvendha Velaan Cholan (Uththama Cholan). Besides, they also fixed the rates of taxation to be paid by all the 18 subjects.

A charter from the era of King Kulothunga Chola I states that a left-hand versus right-hand castes riot broke out at Rajamahendra Chaturvedi Mangalam. The riot arose the second year after the king ascended the throne. The entire village was burnt down. The temple seer and the idols were looted. The things that escaped their plunder could also not be preserved. T.N. Subramanian, the author of *South Indian Temple Inscriptions,* mentions the following about the riot:

> There has been a long-standing hostility between the left-hand and right-hand caste clusters. The encounter was primarily for certain rights in their social life. Sometimes, peace deals were reached. But they were based on the rights enjoyed by specific clusters.

Some charters list a few right-hand and left-hand castes. While closely observing these charters, we understand that the Valangaiyar (right-hand) castes owned fertile or arid lands, whereas the Idangaiyar (left-hand) castes were connected to trade or skilled occupations. Smiths such as Thachchan, Chetti, Seniyan, and Kaikolan were the Idangaiyar castes. Landowning castes such as Pallar and Paraiyar were Valangaiyar castes.

Landlords headed the right-hand castes and lived off the labour of those who worked on their land. Wealthy merchants were the leaders of the left-hand caste and lived by exploiting the artisans' labour. In socio-political struggles for supremacy, the landlords enlisted the right-hand castes and attacked the merchants; meanwhile, the merchants enlisted the left-hand castes. To resist the merchants' collective exploitation, the landlords ensured the working class remained divided, prompting minor clashes among the artisans.

Looking at the above charters, it is clear that the left-hand castes fought against unjust taxes and social oppression. The upper castes stirred up caste divisions and conflicts so that the lower castes within their right-hand caste cluster would not unite with the left-hand castes based on their similar class. The Brahmins frequently provided new narratives for such caste divisions. So, these divisions were not created by the Brahmins but rather by the upper class to protect their interests (material possessions). However, the Brahmins, through their excellent source of knowledge, were instrumental in documenting Puranas and other law books to protect the interests of these classes.

Varuna Sinthamani, which explains the feudal pride of the Velaalar, elaborates on the left and right caste divisions and narrates the following story.

Madana Boopathi, a tyrant and lustful man, ruled the city of Kanchi. He forced himself on a woman named Vedavalli and raped her. Traumatized by what had happened, she died by suicide. As a result, all the natives left the city. Together, the king and his family perished. Covered with mounds of sand, the country lay deserted without any vegetation.

After a while, Kurumbas, a nomadic pastoral tribe, arrived and settled there with their herds. Later, various masses occupied and established small towns. The communities that had migrated elsewhere – Velaalar, Kavara Chetti, and Vaanigar – returned. Forests turned into a country. The people there could not conduct clan ceremonies due to the lack of governance. They were unable to relish their earnings. They could not engage in business due to burglary, theft, and robbery.

Let us continue the story as presented in *Varuna Sinthamani*:

> At that time, the wise people thought that if we all got together and established a leader among us and gave him the power to conduct world affairs and make arrangements to follow his orders, we could live peacefully in this place. This would be good. They all collectively consented to execute this idea.
>
> Everyone was happy to hear this. When asked where to identify such a person with all the good qualities, one replied that one could find semblance to these qualities in a person from the Velaan (peasant) community. We know that the residents of this village have the unique ability to live in the middle of the land, avoid enmity, protect the people from hatred, be independent and respect the land, and cultivate their character.
>
> The community gathered and deliberated for some time and unanimously agreed that the Velaalar possessed all these qualities. They identified a noble person from the Velaalar community with all the virtues. They decided he would be their leader and

> exercise authority over the masses, giving him the title 'Mudaliar.'[49] The legacy of this name continues to date. (Pillai)

The Kammalar who heard this narrative envied the Velaalar and questioned if they had to be subservient to them. They realized that they could not win against the Velaalar. They devised a strategy to create a ruckus, establish divisions among people, and pursue their goal of grabbing the power given to the Velaalar. They called out to the commercial Chettis and instigated them, triggering their ego by questioning their subservience to the Velaalar. The commercial Chettis inquired about the change in the status quo. The Kammalar responded that if the Chettis were ready to spend some capital, they would ensure that the power given to the Velaalar could be reversed and the Chettis' rule would prevail. The Chettis were coaxed into becoming the masters of the community, and, in turn, they spent lavishly. The Kammalar bribed some of the spokespersons of their community, asking them to convince the masses to hand over the leadership to the Chettis. Some agreed while others disagreed, resulting in two factions emerging amongst the masses.

The groups that wanted the Velaalar to continue their governance were: Kavaraigal, Reddys, Kammavaaru, Konthalavar, Naththamaan, Malayamaan, Komutti, Idayar, Saaliyar, Seniyar, Pattu Noorkaarar, Sedar, Sekku Vaaniyar, Eruththu Vaaniyar, Ilai Vaaniyar, Janappar, Muchchiliyar, Kaanchiyaar, Vedagaarar, Josiyar, Kuyavar, Melakarar, Nattuvar, Dasis, Eettiyar, Kuravar, Sukkaar, Lambadis, Vettaikaarar, Pattanavar, Ottavar, Upparavar, Pogi, Pani Seyvor, Vannar, Navithar, Poosaari, Irular, Parayar, and Vettiyaan.

The groups that wanted the Chettis, a commerce-oriented group, to take over the power of governance from the Velaalar were Kaikolar, Kammalar, and Pallis. Since the groups that supported the Velaalar were strong, they came to be called Valangai (right-hand), and the groups that supported the Chettis were weak and hence were called Idangai (left-hand). Since the Velaalar group emerged stronger, governance remained with them. The popularity, integrity, and might of the Velaalar are mentioned below:

> Since the Velaalar did not join hands with either group, they remained neutral. Subsequently, the Kavarai Mudaliar supported the leadership of

Velaalar; they took pride in associating themselves with the Velaalar as *Valangaiyar* (right-hand caste cluster). In such a context, the Kammalar vowed revenge against the Velaalar. Meanwhile, the Kammalar made the tools and instruments required for the agricultural use of the Velaalar and were unhappy about the Velaalar dominance over them. Challenging the power of the Velaalars, they grew arrogant and boycotted their occupation. The villagers could not perform their agricultural work due to the lack of instruments, so they took the matter to the leader, who put the Kammalar behind bars. At once, the Kammalar womenfolk approached the leader. They promised to make the necessary instruments and requested the release of their husbands. In that fashion, the Kammalar womenfolk made agricultural instruments for several days. The Kammalar men sided with the Idangaiyar, and their women sided with the Valangaiyar. Unable to stay behind bars for several days, they agreed to take up their profession without disruption and pleaded with the leader to release them. They were released from prison and, subsequently, continued their regular work. Moreover, like the Kammalars,

> the other communities continued their work without interruption; the leader governed the people for a long time, rendering justice to the righteous. The land grew prosperous. (Pillai)

The Velaalars governance wrote this legend to exhibit their merit. The story exaggerates their superiority and excellence. There is no documented evidence for many of the events told as historical facts in this story, nor is there any evidence regarding them in the stories narrated by the other castes of the region. For example, the period in which this story is said to have occurred is the period of the ancient Cholas. There is no evidence to support the existence of left- and right-caste divisions at that time. There is no record to support that there were officers such as governors and commanders in the history of the Chola dynasty. It was only during the later Chola period, those who worked under the king's command were given the titles such as governors, commanders, and officials. The charters of the last Chola dynasty addressed the left-hand and right-hand caste clusters, as well as the conflicts and riots that broke out between the two groups. The charter details the names of those castes. References to the landowning aura of the Valangaiyar and the trade and artisan connectivity of the Idangaiyar castes have been cited earlier. But in this story, many more caste names are considered Valangai castes, contrary to the evidence. Besides, during the later Chola period, the period in which the events of the story are said to have taken place, the names of caste groups that spoke Telugu such as Kavarais, Reddys, Kammavaaru, and Komutti were not counted among the Valangai castes. Also, the list mentions castes engaged in handicrafts as Valangai castes.

Despite all these contradictions, the core of this story is a social reality. Among the Velaalars, it is a fact that the landlords were state officials, and their dominance was opposed by the merchant group, the Chettiars. The Chettiars fought to expand the social base to protect their interests by recruiting their associates. The Idangaiyar fought against the landlords as they had political dominance. Their leaders, the Chettis, fought for trade rights, tax concessions, abolition of customs duties, etc. The industrialists who stood with them for tax reduction fought for certain rights that indicated social status.

Landlords used their positions of power to protect

their interests and maintain the social order. Details from the charters clarify this premise. As a result of their revolt, King Kulothunga Cholan I accepted the merchants' demands and waived off customs duty. Hence the King was known by the epithet 'King Who Abolished Tax', which finds a reference in 'Kalingathupparani' (a twelfth century war song by Jayamkondar) and 'Meikeerthi' (translated as 'true fame', and found in the inaugural portion of Tamil inscriptions, as evidenced by charters traced from ancient Chola monarchs). Idangai castes also received some concessions from him from time to time.[50]

It is this social truth that the story tells differently, in a way that favours them. Therefore, the landowners and merchants in the history of social development created the right-hand and left-hand caste factions to draw people to their side for their vested interests.

The Velaalars, the landed gentry, called the sects that supported them as Valangaiyars (right-hand caste cluster) but also maintained that they did not belong to the caste. They could not admit they were one of the Valangai castes who fought for them; why? Parayar and Kuravar were among those who supported them. Brahmins do not belong to any cluster. The Velaalars claim this to project that they were superior like the

Brahmins and not did not permit others to perceive that they were part of a confederacy that included lower-caste sections. However, their caste, too, belongs to the Valangai division.

Velaalars and Brahmins collected evidence of their caste superiority and wrote stories. Meanwhile, at the same time, they wrote in these stories that the people belonging to the left and right castes were subordinate to them. For example, stories suggest that the Velaalars were the sons of Ganga, the Nadars were the sons of Shakti Muni, and when Sage Kashyap came to the South, the Idangai were born from his ear ornament and carried his sandals.[51]

Considering the perspectives fictionalized by the Brahmins favouring the landlords and themselves, Markasagayam Aasaari states that the Brahmins created the left-hand and right-hand caste distinction.

The above evidence establishes that the Kammalar developed their perspectives on their struggles towards caste equality.

1. They use the Yajur Veda to claim their emanation (creation) from the Panchamuga Brahma (five-faced Brahma). They say castes are equal because all professions are creations of Brahma.
2. They argue that labour is the cause of the

world's salvation, and those who labour are the descendants of Lord Brahma.

3. They object and reject referring to labour as menial.
4. They say all the Puranas are false because they display different accounts of Thirumurthy's (God) appearance.
5. They also use the Rig Veda, which advocates human equality when castes did not exist, to develop their ideas of caste equality.
6. Although they claim the Puranas as false, since the Brahmins use the Puranas as a source of caste hierarchy, the origin of the rishis – the patriarchs of the Brahmins – is associated with a low caste, and they use the same Puranas to show that the Brahmins belong to the Shankara caste. Further, they establish that the Brahmins cannot deny this fact.
7. After establishing caste hierarchy (superiority and lowliness), Manusmriti proposes that the varna system maintains the moral rules of the caste order, so they oppose it.
8. Since the Shudras consider labour as consciousness and are the best amongst the clans as they feed everyone, they say that they, too, have the right to read wisdom texts such as the Vedas.

9. They use 'Kabilaragaval', which strongly advocates the principles of caste equality, to defend their views. Non-Brahmin upper castes, such as Velaalar and Karkathar, agree with the section of the song that opposes Brahmin ascendancy. However, they disagree that humanity should not be differentiated based on caste. They consider that there should not be a caste above them. However, they are not ready to step down from their position to admit that there is no superiority or inferiority amongst castes.

Enclosure

('Kabilaragaval' is a significant text in the context of this essay since it was a well-thought-out song that critiques the caste system. By alluding to the various texts in this essay, Na. Va. brings to light the importance of rejecting caste and highlights the realities of this illogical practice.)

'Kabilaragaval'

(This extract begins at line number 57 and continues till the end of the poem.)

THE *Brahmins extended the sacred texts*
The dead were buried here
Adorning recitals were repeated
Angavar recovered from collapsing hunger
When you are fed by the sons of the dead ancestors
Were the hungry ancestors seen stretching out their hands for food?
Whose hunger was satiated by the food consumed?
Scavengers, Barbarians, Foreigners, Sinhalese,
Slender-waisted Lankan Moors, Sculptors, and Chinese
There are no Brahmins in these countries.
Just like no other principle in the order of creation
You established the four-pronged caste order.
Impressed the need for higher and lower order.
The cow and the buffalo are distinct in their birth
Have you not seen an offspring born
Of copulation between a man and a woman of two different castes?
And the offspring came to be called a caste
Let that be.
Like a red water lotus blooming in the mud
Vasishtan was taken to a stranger of his concubine
Saththiyar was taken to Vasishtar of Sandali
Parasara was borne to Saththiyar of Pulaichi

Vyasar was delivered to Parasara in the womb of a fisherwoman
Aren't these four who recited the Vedas and advanced as sages?
No matter what seed is planted in any land
It sheds its skin and sprouts
Boosurar (the Brahmin) copulated
With a Pulaichi and bore a child.
Is it unusual to be born someone else?
Isn't the born child a Boosuran?
We know that the cow and the buffalo are distinct
But who has seen such distinctions in humans?
Lifetime – organs
Consonant (organ within the body) – sense-knowledge
The difference is not evident in any of these, too.
A Pulayan born in the South
He goes North and recites without guilt
He becomes a Brahmin (seer)
A Brahmin (seer) moves Southward from the North
And becomes a Pulayan through his behavioural change. Let that be.
Like a red water lotus blooming in the mud
Vasishtan was taken to a stranger of his concubine
Saththiyar was taken to Vasishtar of Sandali

Parasara was borne to Saththiyar of Pulaichi
Vyasar was delivered to Parasara in the womb of a fisherwoman
Aren't these four who recited the Vedas and advanced as sages?
Austere ascetic Kabilar
I am Kabilar borne of Aadhi, a Pulaichi
Seven other offsprings other than me
Three men and four women
Let me narrate a bit about this.
Uppai grew up in the washerfolk household at Oothukaadu
Uruvai grew up in the palm-picking Sandror family in the toddy-selling slum of Kaveripoompattinam
Auvai grew up in the harp-reviving Panar household
Valli grew up in the millet-growing family of Kuravar
Valluvar grew up in the mountain regions of Thondai Nadu, in the home of Mayilai Paraya
Adhiyaman grew up in the Vanchi kingdom
I, Kabilar, grew up in the Haaroor Brahmin household.
So, will rain leave a few and only fall on some people?
Or the wind blows only for a few, leaving out some people?
Or does the land not bear some people?

Or does the Sun not give heat and light to some people?
Do the upper castes get food from the country, and the lower castes from the forest?
Gaining wealth or going poverty-stricken
Meditating and dying, humans are no different
Clan, section, death, or birth – it's the same for all.
God is one for all; it is in one's mind.
Therefore, the precepts of the ancestors should be followed
On any given day, one must be gracious to the bereaved
Contempt, murder, and theft must be avoided
Remain virtuous, apart from male and female distinction
There must be no discrimination
Moral, excellence, and generosity alone lead to goodness
Birth doesn't render good; realize this foolish Brahmin.

A brief explication of 'Kabilaragaval'

'Kabilaragaval', or 'Kabilar Agaval', attributed to Kapiladeva Nayanar, is a notable Tamil text from the fifteenth century, belonging to the genre of Agaval, one of the four principal verse forms in medieval

Tamil Nadu. This text espouses a critical perspective on the caste system and can be construed as a treatise grounded in rationality. The narrative posits the birth of seven individuals, four girls and three boys, to a high-caste sage named Bhagavan and a low-caste woman named Adi. They were respectively Uppai (born in the house of Vannar in Oothukaadu), Uruvai (born in the house of Sandror in Kaveripoompattinam), Auvai (born in the house of Panar), Valli (born in the house of Malai Kuravar), Valluvar (born in the house of Paraiyar in Mailai), Adhiyaman (born in the house of Vanchi), and Kabilar (born in the house of the Brahmin seer in Aurur). It is important to note that scholars generally consider this narrative a work of fiction. The text emphatically asserts the transcendence of caste for both God and learned sages.

TAMIL KINGS AND CASTE DIVISIONS

INSCRIPTIONS FROM THE TIME OF THE CHOLA DYNASTY reveal the existence of two predominant caste clusters. The records from the rule of King Rajarajan I enumerate caste groupings as follows: Valangai Pazham Padaikalilar (right-hand caste cluster), Perundanaththu Valangai Perum Padaigal (right-hand upper castes of Perundanaththu), Azhagiya Chozhath Therintha Valangai Velaikkaara Padaigal (right-hand labour class cluster chosen by the Majestic Chola), and Rajarajan Therintha Valangai Velaikkaarar (right-hand labour class under the direct supervision of King Rajarajan).

Following King Rajarajan's era, inscriptions excavated thereafter during the Chola reign note that the Idangai group (left-hand castes groups) were said to be a composite of ninety, ninety-six and ninety-eight castes. These inscriptions document caste clusters such as Idangai Thonnootraaru (a cluster of ninety-six castes under the left-hand group) and Idangai Thonnootruettu Samaya Thodagai (a sect of ninety-eight religious communities under the left-hand group). Subsequent inscriptions from the later Chola period feature similar nomenclature, such as Moondrukai Magaasenai (Triadic Mega Army[1]) and Moondrukai Thiruvelaikaarar (Triadic King-chosen Executors[2]). Contemplating whether these triads were organized by caste or class prompts thoughtful consideration. To answer this query accurately, it is crucial to delve into the constituent castes of these three clusters (left-hand caste group, Triadic Mega Army, and Triadic King-chosen Executors), their respective occupations, and the interconnections they maintained.

The Valangai group (right-hand cluster) comprised of landowners, peasants, and labourers such as Vannan,[3] Navithan,[4] Vanniyar,[5] and Idayar.[6] Besides Tamil Nadu, these castes also held prominence in the Telugu- and Kannada-speaking areas. In a verdict offered in 1879 for the Madras Municipal Corporation, Justice George Coleman pronounced the names of certain castes within this cluster, relying on evidence from inscriptions and copper charters dating back a little over a century and a half: Kusavan,[7] Melakarar,[8] Sanan,[9] Ambattar[10], Kannan (a sub-caste within Kammalar community), Idaiyan (same as Idayar), Vellalan,[11] Parayan,[12] Kuravar,[13] Ottan,[14] Irulan,[15] Vedan,[16] Vettuvan,[17] etc. Based on the available evidence, the right-hand cluster encompassed landowning freeholders and cultivators who worked on lands owned by freeholders aided by labourers.

Likewise, existing records indicate that the left-hand cluster encompassed either ninety-six or, in some accounts, ninety-eight castes. Written during Veerarajendra Chola's rule, the Thiruvenkadu inscription[18] outlines the taxes collected by the king from castes belonging to the left-hand cluster, which were subsequently offered to the temple. The castes mentioned in this inscription were traders, artisans, Thachchan (carpenters), and Karuman (blacksmiths). Edgar Thurston,[19] a scholar, listed the ensuing castes as part of the left-hand group: traders and artisans, carpenters and blacksmiths. Further, he mentioned the following castes as belonging to the left-hand group: Chetti,[20] Vaniyan (astronomers), Devangan,[21] Koththan (masons), Thattan (goldsmiths), Kannan,[22] Kollan (blacksmiths), Sakkiliyan,[23] etc.

Detailed information about the Triadic Mega Army, similar to the records available for the right-hand and left-hand caste groups, is inaccessible. No evidence has been found to indicate that the Triadic Mega Army adhered to the caste system similar to the right-hand and left-hand clusters. This third cluster of people (the Triadic Mega Army), distinct from the right-hand and left-hand caste clusters, may be considered the King's cluster, where everyone was treated equally. Hence, this essay confines itself to elucidating the relationship between the right-hand and left-hand clusters in the context of the King's rule. The following explanation addresses the concerns previously raised in this essay.

In the previous essay, we gained an understanding of how the Chola regime primarily operated on a system (tax levy) that exploited land tenure.[24] To sustain this system of exploitation, the rulers needed to establish a solid social base (monetary in the form of taxation) within the kingdom. With this base, they could exploit the populace within the kingdom or wage wars beyond its borders. Therefore, they strategically offered concessions in the taxes imposed at various junctures to gain the support of different groups.

For the first time, extensive pieces of land were

allocated to temples, but the supervision was entrusted to the landowners themselves to safeguard land holding. Among the landowners in a village, the caste with the largest population formed the village council and administrative assembly, overseeing the lands critical to the king's social foundation. However, the number of landowners was relatively sparse. As a result, the king extended certain privileges to the labouring class in exchange for their support. Caste groups not directly involved in agricultural labour such as Vannar, Ambattar, Melakarar, thus received benefits. Nevertheless, the riot that broke out during that era between the left-hand and right-hand clusters suggests substantial exploitation of land tenure.

However, if the kingdom incurred losses due to concessions granted to landowners and peasants, it was compensated by imposing additional taxes on merchants and their labourers. For instance, taxes were levied on a range of high-value commercial goods such as pearls, ivory, coral, areca nuts, sandalwood, cardamom, granite, clothing, and silk, dating back to the reign of King Rajarajan. Merchant groups such as Valanjiyam, Manigiramam, Nanadesi, Nagarathar, etc., have had to pay taxes since ancient times.

Numerous stone inscriptions have recorded various taxes, including Agavai (house tax), Ugavai (money tax), Ottachchu (an ancient levy), Paai (tax on water transportation), Thari (tax on looms), Erai (an ancient form of taxation), Tattar-pattam (tax on goldsmiths), etc., collected from individuals engaged in trade and their labourers.

As trade prospered, the influence of merchant clusters grew. They recognized that abolishing these taxes would further enhance their business. To achieve this goal, they sought a popular uprising, enlisting the support of labourers (Kammalar)[25] involved in their trade – including the manufacturers of commercial goods. Details of the rebellion are mentioned in the stone inscriptions excavated from the Chola dynasty.

While the landowning classes and their allied castes constituted the right-hand cluster, the merchant class and their associate castes emerged as the left-hand cluster. When the right-hand faction was financially strong, the king joined hands with them and subdued the left-hand section. Likewise, when the left-hand faction grew more potent and robust, the king offered them a few concessions.

For example, during the reign of Kulothunga

Cholan I, the merchant clusters developed trade and commercial ties with countries such as Sri Lanka, Sumatra, Java, and Burma; they gained great wealth and influence. Meanwhile, war after war emptied the king's treasury. The king refrained from imposing further taxes to avoid the merchant classes' remonstrance. He used a trick to increase their income and earn himself money. The taxes levied on exported goods were lifted, which pleased the merchants. Their profits grew exponentially, and they even gifted a portion to the king. The king gained their support in this fashion. This information is found in Kulothungan's inscriptions and Ottakoothar's[26] *Kulothungan Ula* ('The Procession of Kulothungan').[27]

The Manadu[28] inscription states thus: 'A supremo who excluded taxes and reduced the burden.'

Similarly, *Kulothungan Ula* states: 'Emperor Rajarajan waived the taxes during his reign.'

The occupational characteristics of individuals within the left-hand and right-hand clusters engendered disparities in their well-being. Both cultivators in the right-hand cluster and labourers in the left-hand cluster experienced commensurate hardship resulting from the exploitative land tenure policies imposed by the king. The king deliberately fomented dissent by exploiting and exposing age-old duels, preventing the groups from forming a united front against their oppressive rule. Historians state that these riots are addressed as left-hand versus right-hand caste unrest, and such clashes blew out owing to convoluted perspectives about the superiority of one group as opposed to the other. One of the inscriptions from Aduthurai[29] refers to the revolts between the left-hand and right-hand clusters. T.N. Subramanian refers to this through the following inscription:

> Landowning communities, such as the Vanniyar, the Velaalar,[30] and the Brahmins, united to cause injustices to the ninety-six castes in the left-hand cluster, helped by officials in the kingdom. Similarly, inscriptions excavated from several places in the State refer to the tax burden the left-hand castes bore.[31]

Therefore, petty caste disputes were not the reasons for these continuous revolts but injustices meted out by the right-hand castes. While the king encouraged these injustices on the weak left-hand cluster, he offered them a few concessions when they grew strong en masse.

The king and the landowning communities tried to create trivial fights within the left-hand cluster. When these attempts were successful, left-hand castes were vehemently subdued, and their taxes increased. Realizing the need for unity through experience, the left-hand cluster stayed united, as referred to in the Valikandapuram[32] inscription. The inscription states:

> In the inscription of Emperor of Swasthisree Thiribhuvanam, King Rajarajan, in the sixteenth year at Vadakarai Naattu Valikandapuram, in the Thiruvaliswaram Nayanar Temple that hosts all the left-hand groups, stipulates that everybody will share the good and bad fortune of the members: communities from various regions composed of Brahmins, Chitrameli Periya Naattaar,[33] Yadava,[34] Malayaman (chieftains), Kayangudi Brahmins, and Paravar.[35] Through this inscription, ordinary folks have expressed their consideration to partake in the better and worse of each individual from their left-hand cluster and different castes referred to in it. Having promised to adhere to this pact, if anyone goes against it, he will be degraded lower than others and the lowly castes.[36]

The latter part of the above inscription defines the fine imposed on those who violate this verdict.

This inscription advocates unity among the Idangai groups and encourages members of the Valangai groups, including Periya Naattaar, Yadava, Paravar, etc., to unite in solidarity against malevolent forces. It reflects the collective resolve of ordinary people, expressing the belief that any individual's experiences, whether positive or negative, should be perceived and shared by all.

Most attempts by the kings to pit both caste groups against each other and prolong their exploitations were successful. After suffering many tribulations in public, the labour communities from the right-hand cluster promised to unite to resist evil and welcome goodness. The Valikandapuram inscription is historically significant and exposes the reality of caste practices.

These rare shreds of evidence make it safe to conclude that the riots between the left-hand and the right-hand groups were not mere caste riots but confederations of factions joined by landowning castes and the mercantile class, a clash due to class antagonism. We understand that the labour class of the lower strata from both clusters deliberately stood away and attempted to resist evil and welcome goodness.

NOTES

Editorial to the First Edition (1980)

1. Na. Vanamamalai, *Marxist Aesthetics* (Chennai: People's Publishing House, 1978), 8.

Perspectives on Caste and Equality Struggles in Tamil Nadu

1. Castes in the Sangam Age were based on occupation. *Purananooru* is a collection of four hundred heroic poems composed by 157 poets and poetesses that addressed the issue of caste. The last of the eight anthologies of Sangam literature In the preface to *Purananooru*: *Sources and Notes*, U.V. Saminathaiyer provides a list of castes. The names that appear in his list of castes serve as proof of this truth about castes:

Anthanar (Brahmin), Arasar (king), Alavar (cultivator), Eyavar (drummer/one who plays skinned instruments), Idayar (shepherd/herdsman), Uppu Vanigar (salt merchant), Umanar (salt maker), Uzhavar (farmer/ploughman/cultivator), Aeitriyar, Kadambar, Kadai Siyar, Kammiyar, Kalamar (farmer/field-toiler), Kinaignar, Kinai Magal, Kuyavar (pot maker), Kurathiyar, Kuravar, Kurumban, Kooththar, Kollar (artisan/smith), Thachchar (carpenter), Therppaagar (charioteer), Thudiyar, Nulaiyar, Bharatavar (fisher folk), Paraiyar, Padini, Panar (bard/minstrel), Paanichchi, Pulayar, Poonsey Kollar, Pothu Vilai Magalir (sex workers), Porunar, Madayar, Mazhavar, Yaazh Pulavar, Yaanaip Paagar, Yaanai Vaettuvar, Vannaathi (washer-woman), Vanigar, Vilaignar, Vilaippendir, and Vedar (hunter).

2. Poetry as early as the Sangam period provides references to the existence of the fourfold caste-based social structure. *Silappathikaram* (The Tale of an Anklet) is one of the five great ancient Tamil epics by Ilango Adigal. Commentary on the varna elements in the *Silappathikaram* (a historical epic that addresses the integrity of Kovalan and the wrath of Kannagi that

burnt the city of Madurai due to a false pronouncement of the king) shows the validity of this notion.

3. Puliyur Kesigan. *Thirukkural: New Prose Text* (Chennai: Poombukar Publications, 2010), 203.
4. Apart from the stories on caste history narrated later, Robert Hart Grave, in the *Journal of Tamil Studies* (May 1969, Volume 1-Issue 1), discussed the caste history of the Nadar. He analyzed the caste stories of the Nadar written by the Christians of Tirunelveli (between 1851–1918) and *The History of Nadars* by Sargunam. These stories and texts have tried to prove that they hail from the lineage of the Pandya kings/rulers.
5. These perspectives can be found in the texts written by Manonmaniam Sundaram Pillai (a nineteenth century Indian scholar who wrote the famous play Manonmaniyam and the state anthem of Tamil Nadu, the *Thamizh Thaai Vazhthu*), Maraimalai Adigal (a nineteenth century Tamizh Shaivaite, he was a Tamil orator, writer and the father of the Pure Tamizh Movement; he and his followers attribute his efforts to the Self-Respect Movement), V.P. Subbiramaniya Mudaliar (Vellakal Palaniapa Subramania Mudaliar, a nineteenth century translator who translated books

on veterinary diseases from English to Tamil. He had his Tamil, English, and Veterinary education. King George V gave him the title Rao Shaib in 1926 for his contributions in the field of medicine.), and C. K. Subramaniya Mudaliar (C.K.S, a distinguished Tamil scholar of the nineteenth century, played a pivotal role in disseminating Shaivite devotion during the twentieth century. Notably, he authored an exhaustive treatise on the Periya Puranam, a work that holds a prominent position in Tamil literature and occupies a significant role within the theological framework of Shaivism.).

6. Kadalur Kanagasabai Pillai. *Varuna Sinthamani.* (Chennai: Alpiniyan Press, 1901). Wealthy folks from the Velaalar castes donated to get this book published. This information is stated in the preface of the book.]
7. Ibid.
8. Ibid. Chapters 1, 3, and 7.
9. T. V. Duraisamy Giramani. *The Kshatriya Clan: An In-depth Overview* (Chennai: Progressive Press, 1904).
10. Gurukkal, Ramalinga and V. A. Kumarayya Nadar. *Nadar Mannarum Nayakka Mannarum* [*Nadar Kings and Nayaka Kings*]. Chennai: Sachidanandam Press, 1937.

11. 'Kabilaragaval' [Tamil Nool Nilayam, 1940]. The part about caste equality in this hymn is added as a postscript. From available charters, we comprehend that hierarchically inferior castes fought lawsuits against each other to gain a few rights for themselves. The exact details of the rights are unavailable. But the charters mention a few. For example, lawsuits have been fought for rights such as the number of awnings, the number of umbrellas to be held in the wedding procession, the number of conches to be blown, the number of instruments to be played, the number of drums to be played, the number of conches blown in death rituals, the number of pitchers to bring water in, and whether to pave the footpath with a carpet or not.
12. An Asura king
13. Ancient Tamil Assemblies
14. Yama, the King
15. Eelam in the Tamil original. Refers to present-day Sri Lanka
16. Ravanan
17. Sri Lanka
18. Vishnu
19. Vaishyas

20. Ibid.
21. A sect of Brahmins
22. Seven Virgins
23. Guru Muni is a reference to the dwarfish sage, Agastya, one of the prominent figures portrayed in the Puranas, is a Siddha, who is recognized as the embodiment of nine celestial beings that descended to Earth to enlighten humanity.
24. Agastheeswaram Arumuga Nadar. *Kaliyaana Vaazhthu* (Wedding Greetings). (Kanya Kumari: Self-published, 1977). Songs from the *Kaliyaana Vaazhthu* section are found in the Nadar folk songs compiled by Agastheeswaram Arumuga Nadar.
25. Arulappa Mudaliar. *Paravar Puranam* (Legends of the Fisherfolk). (Chennai: Mayyanban Tamil Research Centre, 1909]. This information about the six wealthy folks from the Bharata clan (fisherfolk) who donated to publish the text is found in the preface of the above text.
26. Urvashi is a creation of Narayana, the slap on his thigh birthed her; In Sanskrit, Uru refers to thigh, and she bore the name Urvashi; Pururavan fell in love with her
27. The daughter of Asura king Vrishaparva and Yayati fell in love with her.

28. Indirakulam (Indira clan) refers to the lineage of Indran son of Kashyapa, one of the seven rishis.
29. The celestial kingdom of Indiran
30. Caste-historical folk songs about Pallars are only partially available. However, the third collection of 'South Indian Temple Charters' was compiled by T.N. Subramanian and it reports the king's verdict in the cases regarding the rights of Pallars and Paraiyars during the Tirumala Nayakkan period. The stories in the charter must have been based on the historical traditions handed down by the Pallars.
31. Debi Prasad Chattopadhyay. *Lokayatha: A Study in Ancient Indian Materialism.* (Chennai, People's Publishing House, 1959).
32. R. Venkatachalam Pillai. *Manimegalai*, (Chennai: The South India Saiva Siddhanta Works Publishing Society, 1946), 13.
33. K. Appadurai Pillai. *Neelagesi*, [Chennai: The Balussery Press, 1955], Synopsis of the Vedas. *Neelagesi* is one of the five minor epics by a Jain saint, Vaamanar, a counter to Buddhist arguments. The title translates as *Woman with Blue Hair*.
34. In the era of King Ukkira Peruvazhuthiyar of the Pandya dynasty, there lived a devout Chozhiya Brahmin named

Aadhi. He married a maiden from Karuvoor and they had seven children together – four girls and three boys. Aadhi, however, decided to leave each child in the locality where they were born. Consequently, the children were brought up in the households of their respective birthplaces and were recognized as members of the castes of the families that raised them.

35. Tiruvenkata Mudaliar. *Judgment of Adalat Court, Chittoor*, (Chennai: Iyatramil Vilakka Achchu, 1924). The previous edition of this book was published much earlier. Kanniya Pillai published the second edition in response to the Chennai Brahma Sabha. These details are available in the preface of this reference text.
36. T.N. Subramanian. *South Indian Temple Inscriptions.* (Chennai: Government Oriental Manuscripts Library, 1957), xiii.
37. The practice of Idangai, or the left-hand division, in Tamil Nadu, represents a historical caste-based stratification persisting from ancient times until the nineteenth century, with remnants enduring into the early decades of the twentieth century AD. The Idangai segment, constituting a numerical minority, comprised occupational communities engaged in manufacturing activities such as metalworking and weaving. The

primary constituents of the Idangai grouping were the five castes collectively known as Anchalar/ Panchalar, namely Kannar, Thattar, Aasaari, Kollar, and Thachchan. Additional castes were subsequently incorporated into the Idangai cluster at various junctures.

38. T.N. Subramanian. *South Indian Temple Inscriptions.* (Chennai: Government Oriental Manuscripts Library, 1957).
39. Pillai, Gudalur Kanagasabai. *Varuna Sinthamani* [Varna Manual]. (Chennai: Alpiniyan Press, 1901), The chapter 'Who are the Shudras?' in *Varuna Sinthamani.*
40. The Yajur Veda talks about the production of Panchamuga Brahma. It describes the creative power as Vishwa Brahma, its five manifestations as Panchamuga Brahma (five-faced Brahma), and states that the five rishis appeared individually as demigods of these occupations.
41. Gundaiyan states that occupations using iron, copper, stone, wood, etc., were deemed disgraceful (disgusting). According to the plaintiffs, the manufacturing and copper industries function similarly to the occupations mentioned above. Markasagayam Aasaari argues that tools and weapons were quintessential to the day-to-

day livelihood of ordinary folks and the sustenance of kingdoms. He emphasizes that the world revolves around their occupations and believes that their occupations are on par with those performed by Brahma, the Creator God, and Thirumal, the Protector God.

42. The Shatapatha Brahmana and Brihadaranyaka Upanishad provide details of the Sapta (seven) rishis. They are Atri; Bharadvaja; Gautama Maharishi; Jamadagni; Kashyapa; Vasistha; and Vishvamitra.
43. Part of these stories are found in *Manimegalai,* and the rest in 'Kabilaragaval'. *Manimegalai* is one of the five great ancient Tamil epics by Chithalai Satthanar; written as an anti-love story and a sequel to *Silappathikaram* (*Manimegalai* that translates as Jewelled Belt/Girdle of Gems).
44. One of the powerful mantras to God Brahma, and any person who practices this mantra gets material and spiritual benefits if the practitioner appeases God Brahma.
45. The Yajur Veda translation found in this section is from *Varuna Sinthamani.*
46. According to traditional belief, Vishwa Brahmas descended from the five sons of lord Vishwakarma. They are Manu (blacksmith), Maya (carpenter),

Dhuvasta (metal craftsman), Silpi (stone-carver) Vishvajnya (goldsmith).

47. The concept of Valangai, denoting the right-handed faction, delineates a historically prevalent caste-based stratification within communities in the Indian state of Tamil Nadu. This hierarchical division persisted from ancient epochs through the nineteenth century and endured into the early decades of the twentieth century AD. The Valangai faction comprised castes predominantly associated with agrarian pursuits, thus forming a numerical majority in comparison to the Idangai or left-handed faction.
48. T.N. Subramanian. *South Indian Temple Inscriptions.* (Chennai: Government Oriental Manuscripts Library, 1957). [xi-xv].
49. 'Mudaliar' in the Tamil cultural context serves both as an honorific title and a hereditary surname. Its historical connotation denotes its association with individuals of elevated military rank and their progeny, particularly during the governance of the Chola empire.
50. Cholas Ancient Charter, Oriental Manuscripts Library Series. [Kollappa Kanagasabhapathy Pillay, *History of South India.* Palaniappa Brothers, 1960.]

    Professor K.K. Pillai, in his *History of South India*

[Kollappa Kanagasabhapathy Pillay, Palaniappa Brothers, 1960], mentions some of the privileges granted to the lower castes, citing the above charter as evidence:

> Copies of an inscription that details the rights granted by the King to Kammalar are found at Karur, Perur, and Modakkur. The inscription mentions that the King gave the Kammalar certain rights in their wedding ceremonies and caste rituals. The rights include blowing the double conch, beating the drum, wearing sandals, and painting the walls with limestone.

51. K.K. Pillai, South Indian History.

    In ancient times, they started fabricating stories to show that they hailed from superior clans by linking themselves with upper castes. The *Idangai* castes (left-hand castes) made up a story about their Agni Gundam birth. The above information is found in inscriptions from the era of Kulothungan III.

    Each caste created many new fantasy stories to show their caste superiority. They tried to establish themselves as equal to the Brahmins. Against this, the Brahmins, too, made up stories that show other castes as subordinate to theirs. The *Idangai* caste (left-hand castes) could not have written the story of Agni

Gundam. Instead of elevating their status, it lowers the left-hand caste cluster as sandal-bearers of the Brahmins. Brahmins must have written this story to establish their superiority over others.

Tamil Kings and Caste Divisions

1. Bands of horses, chariots, and elephants.
2. The workers who carried the king's order without a second thought and executed as ordered.
3. Vannan, also Vannar, is a caste group in Tamil Nadu and north-eastern Sri Lanka. They have traditionally been involved in washing laundry and worked as agricultural labourers.
4. See Ambattar for reference to Navithar/Navithan.
5. Vanniyar/Vanniyan, also called Palli/Padayatchi, were soldiers or warriors during the time of the Chola dynasty. The Vanniyars typically worked as small-scale farmers tending to modest plots of land or as laborers without any land holdings.
6. Idayar, also known as Konar/Ayar, are a part of the Yadava community that primarily engages in cattle herding and cultivation.
7. Potters/Pot-makers in Tamil Nadu.

8. This caste group is a conglomerate with a few other castes, broadly called the Isai Vellalar community in Tamil Nadu. It has a longstanding tradition of engaging in classical dance and music performances within Hindu temples and the courts of their benefactors. Isai Vellalar encompasses individuals with minstrel occupations such as Melakkarar, Nayanakkarar, Nattuvanar, and Vellalar.
9. The Nadar community, also known as Nadan, Shanar, and Shanan, is a prominent Tamil caste in India, primarily concentrated in the districts of Kanyakumari, Thoothukudi, Tirunelveli, and Virudhunagar. Traditionally, most Nadars were involved in the cultivation of palmyra trees and the production of jaggery. Some were also engaged in the toddy trade. Their traditional occupation involved climbing trees to extract the sap from coconuts, which was used in the production of palm wine.
10. The Ambattar, alternatively known as Navithar or Navithan, is a Tamil community primarily found in Tamil Nadu, India and in the north-eastern region of Sri Lanka. Historically, their customary roles have included practicing medicine, serving as midwives, and working as barbers.

11. The Vellalar community comprises various endogamous castes found in Tamil Nadu, Kerala, and the north-eastern regions of Sri Lanka. These include prominent groups like the Arunattu Vellalar, Chozhia Vellalar, Karkatha Velaalar, Kongu Vellalar, Thuluva Vellalar, and the Sri Lankan Vellalar, each with its own distinct identity and cultural practices. They were a prosperous community of farmers and landowners and had more authority, power, and status than the Brahmins in some social and ritual contexts.
12. The Paraiyar, alternatively known as Parayar or Paraiah, is a community residing in Tamil Nadu, Kerala, and Sri Lanka. In the nineteenth century, Robert Caldwell, a missionary and distinguished scholar active in South India, aligned with some contemporary Indian authors in positing that the appellation originated from the Tamil word 'parai', signifying 'drum'. The Paraiyars initially consisted of a guild of percussionists who held a notable function in diverse ceremonial events, including weddings and funerals.
13. The Kuravar are an ethnic community located predominantly in the Kurinji mountainous terrain, spanning the states of Tamil Nadu and Kerala. They bear various appellations in distinct regions of South

India. Additionally, they are identified by a multitude of alternative names, including Malai Kuruvans, Kuravar, Thalaiyaris, Kavalkara Koravars, Uppu Koravars, Dabi Kuravar (Simbu Kuravar), Gandarvakottai Kuravar, Inji Kuravar, Koravas, Kalinji Dabikoravas, and Kala Kuravar.

14. The Waddar community, alternatively referred to as Vodra, Odde, Ottan, or Boyi, is a Hindu caste in India. Originating from the Deccan Plateau, they are primarily associated with the occupation of construction. While Maharashtra is their main demographic stronghold, notable populations are also found in northern Karnataka and Telangana. Traditionally, they engage in various construction-related activities, including stone-crushing, earth-digging, and analogous tasks. Additionally, they partake in well-digging endeavours.
15. The Irula, also known as Irular, constitute a Scheduled Tribe community residing in the northern districts of Tamil Nadu. Their habitat lies near Chennai, a tropical region experiencing seasonal monsoon rains. Linguistically, the Irula language shares roots with Tamil and Kannada, prominent Southern Dravidian languages. In Tamil, the term 'Irula' means 'people of darkness', possibly alluding to their naturally darker complexion or the tradition of conducting significant events under the cover of night.

16. In the 1901 Madras Census Report, the Vedan community was characterized as a Tamil-speaking caste primarily engaged in labour and hunting. Historical records suggest that they originally had a military background, evolving from soldiers to a group with a reputation for engaging in acts of banditry. The term 'Vedan' itself translates to 'hunter'. It's worth noting that in certain regions, this label was sometimes extended to include the Irula community.
17. The Vettuvan community primarily engages in agricultural labour, actively participating in various tasks associated with farming. These tasks encompass ploughing, sowing, weeding, transplanting, water pumping, and harvesting. They predominantly serve as day labourers in the agricultural sector.
18. Thiruvenkadu is a village in Sirkazhi Tahsil in the Mayiladuthurai (Mayavaram) District.
19. Edgar Thurston, (1855–1935), served as the British Superintendent at the Madras Government Museum. His significant contributions encompassed diverse research areas, including zoology, ethnology, and botany in the context of India. In 1909, Thurston authored the comprehensive seven-volume work titled *Castes and Tribes of Southern India*, a pivotal contribution to the Ethnographic Survey of India.

20. The title Chettiar, alternatively spelled as Chetti, Chetty or Shetty, is employed by various trading, weaving, agricultural, and landowning communities in South India, particularly in the states of Tamil Nadu, Kerala, and Karnataka.
21. Devanga, also known as Devala Maharishi, is a sub-caste within Hinduism, primarily associated with the weaving communities in India. They trace their lineage back to Prakrut Brahmins, who were Brahmins by birth. The majority of Devangas are engaged in the craft of weaving silk and cotton fabrics.
22. The Vishwakarma community in India, also known as Vishwa Brahmas, is a social group sometimes characterized as a caste. They assert their status as Brahmins or as holders of a high position in the caste hierarchy, although those outside the community often contest these assertions. This community is further divided into five sub-groups – namely carpenters, blacksmiths, bronze smiths, goldsmiths, and stonemasons. All of them claim descent from Vishwakarma, the revered Hindu deity known as the builder and architect of the heavenly realm.
23. The Arunthathiyar community, primarily located in the Indian state of Tamil Nadu, was officially recognized in

2009 as an inclusive term encompassing various sub-groups, including Chakkiliyar (Sakkiliyar), Madari, Madiga, Pagadai, Thotti, and Adi Andhra communities. Their traditional occupations predominantly revolve around leather and cobbling. Some work as manual scavengers.

24. Na. Vanamamalai refers to his previous essay published in the *Thamarai* [lotus] Volume 2, Issue 5 (April 1960) titled 'Crusades in the Chola Regime.'
25. Kammalar is a caste group in Tamil Nadu and north-eastern Sri Lanka. The Kammalars are involved in crafting. Kammalar is a generic term that comprises Kannar (brass-workers), Kollar (blacksmiths), Tarar (goldsmiths), and Thachchar (carpenters).
26. Ottakoothar was a Tamil poet in the court of later Cholas; Kulothunga Cholan was one among them.
27. *Kulothungan Ula* was written in honour of Kulothunga Cholan.
28. Manadu is a village in the Udangudi block of Thoothukudi (Tuticorin) District.
29. Aduthurai, also called Maruthuvakudi, is a panchayat near Kumbakonam in Thanjavur (Tanjore) District.
30. The term Velaalar is an agricultural community in Tamil Nadu, recognized for their status as one of the earliest

settlers on a global scale. Within the Tamil language, they are denoted as 'Velaalar', which correlates with the equivalent term for agriculture, namely 'velaanmai'.

31. T.N. Subramanian. *South Indian Temple Inscriptions*. (Chennai: Government Oriental Manuscripts Library, 1957).
32. Valikandapuram is a village in Veppanthattai Taluk in Perambalur District.
33. Chitramezhi Periya Nadu constitutes a supra-local assembly, a provincial entity encompassing individuals from twenty-two distinct locales within the Kongunadu region of Tamil Nadu. It predominantly represented the Velaala community, a collective of agriculturists from the eleventh to eighteenth centuries.
34. A pastoral community whose livelihood centres around the raising of cattle.
35. The Paravar community, also called Bharatavar or Bharatakulam and colloquially known as 'Fernando', constitutes a maritime-centric group primarily located in the Indian state of Tamil Nadu and Sri Lanka. The Pandyas, alternatively known as Bharathavars, emerged as the initial seafaring pioneers and rulers, establishing the world's inaugural kingdom.
36. This information is gathered from the Valikandapuram inscription (AR.1943/44-276: AD 1227, Tp)].

BIBLIOGRAPHY

Vanamamalai, Na. *Marxiya Azhagiyal* [*Marxist Aesthetics*]. Chennai: People's Publishing House, 1978.

Kesigan, Puliyur. *Thirukkural: Puthiya Urai* [*Thirukkural: New Prose Text*]. Chennai: Poombukar Publications, 2010.

Saminathaiyer, U.V. *Purananooru: Source and Notes.* Chennai: V.N. Jubilee Printers, 1894.

Thirukudasundaram, K. Ed. *Silappathikaram.* Chidambaram: Annamalai University, 1967.

Venkatachalam Pillai, R. *Manimegalai.* Tirunelveli: The South India Saiva Siddhanta Works Publishing Society, 1946.

Pillai, K. Appadurai *Neelagesi.* Chennai: The Balussery Press, 1955.

Subramanian, T.N. *South Indian Temple Inscriptions.* Chennai: Government Oriental Manuscripts Library, 1957.

Gurukkal, Ramalinga and V.A. Kumarayya Nadar. *Nadar Mannarum Nayakka Mannarum* [*Nadar Kings and Nayaka Kings*]. Chennai: Sachidanandam Press, 1937.

Giramani, Vijaya Duraisamy. *Kshatriya Kula Vilakkam* [*An Illustration of the Kshatriya Clan*]. Chennai: Progressive Press, 1910.

Anonymous. *Kilaivalappamaalai.*

Pillai, Gudalur Kanagasabai. *Varuna Sinthamani* [Varna Manual]. Chennai: Alpiniyan Press, 1901.

Mudaliar, Arulappa. *Paravar Puranam* [*History of the Paravar*]. Chennai: Mayyanban Tamil Research Centre, 1909.

Pandithar, Leon Bharata. *Bharata Pandiyar Varalaaru* [*History of Bharata Pandiya*].

Nadar, Agatheeswaran Arumuga. *Valangaiyar Kadhai* (*Naattu Paada Pradhi*) [*Story of the Right-handed Community* (*manuscript of a folk song*)]. Kanya Kumari: Self-published, 1977.

—— *Vengalarasan Kadhai* (*Naattu Paadal*) [*Story of Vengalaraasan* (*a folk song*)]. Kanya Kumari: Self-published, 1977.

Mudaliar, Thiruvenkata. *Chittoor Adhalaaththu Court Theerpu* [*Chittoor High Court Verdict*]. Chennai: Iyatramil Vilakka Achchu, 1924.

Natarajan, A. *Kabilar Agaval.* Chennai: Tamil Nool Nilayam, 1940.

Historical and Sociological Texts

Hutton, Henry John. *Caste in India: its Nature, Function and Origins.* Bombay: CUP, 1946.

Kosambi, D.D. *An Introduction to the Study of Indian History.* Chennai: Popular Prakashan, 1956.

Nilakanta Sastri, K.A. *The Cholas.* Chennai: University of Madras, 1955.

—— *A History of South India: From Prehistoric Times to the Fall of Vijayanagar.* Chennai: University of Madras, 1958.

Sathyanatha Aiyar, R. *History of Nayaks of Madurai.* Chennai: OUP, 1924.

Pillay, Kolappa Kanakasabhapathy. *Thenninthiya Varalaaru* [*History of South India*]. Chennai: Palaniappa Brothers, 1960.

Philosophy

Chattopadhyay, Debi Prasad. Lokayatha: A Study in Ancient Indian Materialism. Chennai: People's Publishing House, 1959.

—— *Indian Philosophy: A Popular Introduction.* Chennai: People's Publishing House. 1964.

Damodaran, K. *Indian Thought: A Critical Survey.* New Delhi: Asian Publishing House, 1967.

Nilakanta Sastri, K.A. *Development of Religion in South India.* Chennai: Orient Longmans, 1963.

ALSO AVAILABLE FROM HACHETTE INDIA

THE CHARIOT OF WISDOM

SUBRAMANIA BHARATI

SPECIAL BILINGUAL EDITION

Translated and with an introduction by GREGORY JAMES

TAMIL LITERATURE IN ENGLISH TRANSLATION SERIES

Breaking the constraints of style and imagery central to classical Tamil literature, Mahakavi C. Subramania Bharati (1882–1921) heralded a new era for the language by making it simpler, thereby encouraging a wider readership. His prodigious contribution to the writings of his homeland – done while in exile during a tumultuous time in the nation's freedom movement – has since propelled his stature to that of a revered literary figure in the subcontinent.

In *The Chariot of Wisdom*, his only novella, a vexed journalist, plagued by material worries and the daily attrition of twentieth-century, British-occupied India, escapes into a daydream to realms mystical and unexplored. He navigates an imaginary chariot through The World of Tranquillity, The World of Pleasure, The World of Truth and The World of Dharma, and finds his values and ideals informing, competing and often contradicting one another. As his self-doubts deepen, he battles the notion that peace and happiness come at a price.

A critical examination of a colonized, afflicted civilization marred by corruption and greed, Bharati's pioneering work speaks to a morally wounded country through astute observations and lively humour. Translated with refined intellectual acuity by Gregory James, this modern classic – as timely today as it was a century ago – is a cleverly masked plea to the people of a distracted nation to rally together in pursuit of a just society.

For further details and information please visit
www.hachetteindia.com

TAMIL HEROIC POETRY

K. KAILASAPATHY

Foreword by A.R. VENKATACHALAPATHY

An elegant and thorough examination of the riches of Sangam poetry

In this acclaimed comparative study, K. Kailasapathy, the celebrated Sri Lankan academic and critic, introduces and interprets ancient Tamil poems and analyses the stylistic heritage, themes and motifs pervading Sangam poetry while building the literary corpus's bridge to heroic poetry in other languages - most notably Greek. He identifies the formulaic expression, stock phrases and overarching sensibilities pervasive in the poems and, going much against the popular grain, expands on the notion that oral verse-making is central to Sangam poetry.

A nod to Milman Parry, this deeply necessary exploration of our neglected past is an engaging and accessible discourse on one of our most fertile literary ages and, with much agility, connects the dots in studying early Tamil poetry for a modern reader.